The Light Within

Authored by Michael Fitzgibbons

Edited by Nick Yeager

Illustrated by Elizabeth Zwolski

Published November, 2015
ISBN 978-1518642432

For Mary,
For Molly and Joe,
For Michael and Kevin

TABLE OF CONTENTS

PART I: It is Revealed through individuals in the way they live life.

PART II: It is present in the midst of everyday events.

PART III: It is present in our interactions with others.

Foreword

In the second verse of his classic song, "Against the Wind," Bob Seger reflects on his "drifters days," which included "Moving eight miles a minute for months at a time," and "Breaking all the rules that would bend." By the end of the verse, however, Seger finds himself "searching for shelter." And by the end of the song, he realizes that he's "got so much more to think about...what to leave in, what to leave out." I can't think of a more worthwhile "search." In a world that operates at a break-neck pace, often leaving us staggered and looking for what just hit us, it is important for us to consider what is worth keeping, and what is worth letting go. Knowing the difference between the two demands experience, knowledge, maturity, perspective—wisdom.

For as long as I've known him (twenty-three years), Michael Fitzgibbons has always had a certain wisdom about himself. And for as long as I've known him, he has always helped foster those prerequisite qualities in the people he encounters in all walks of his diverse life. Although he wears many hats, at the end of the day, the world is Fitz's classroom, and he is a dynamic educator.

Recently, Fitzgibbons has been working to fit a new hat—poet. And true to his ways, his poetry is energetic and insightful. His poems teach. More specifically, they provide insight into our world by offering us an up-close, introspective view of real people, striking moments, and powerful human interactions. The real beauty of his work lies in the personal lessons that it teaches. His poems allow us the opportunity to take an up-close and personal look at ourselves through the people we encounter in life, the everyday events we experience, and interactions we have with others in our world.

Fitzgibbons believes that we are a people of stories, and a story of people. Our stories are all related—an interwoven, complex system of experiences—and in some sense, our stories are the same. His poems reveal this powerful truth to us. Although he might tell you that his creation process does not include much, if any, consideration of "specific structure," one can plainly see the presence of form and structure in his poems. He masterfully constructs line breaks, using physical spacing across the page to create powerful, often unexpected turns. His poems are rich! His poems are full of meaning! His poems are emotional rollercoasters! His poems take readers on a ride that awakens something in our core. Although his poems challenge us to be honest with ourselves, his free-form narrative style is approachable and fun.

The Light Within is the first collection of poems published by Fitzgibbons. In reading it, we are treated to his unique poetic voice—a voice that has the power to educate us about ourselves, each other, and our world. In short, Fitzgibbons provides us with a beacon of light that illuminates a navigational path through our complex, fast-paced society. After experiencing *The Light Within*, readers will have an easier time answering for themselves Bob Seger's questions about life: "What to leave in?" and "What to leave out?"

Nick Yeager
Editor
Educator and Counselor

ACKNOWLEDGEMENTS

There is absolutely no way I could undertake a project like this without help and inspiration from multiple people and places. Even the first time a friend read one of these poems and said, "Hey, that's really good," it helped push me on the journey to find a voice, if that is indeed what I have finally found.
It helps having a best friend and a wife be the same person. There is so much less to translate when it's only one person. Since I believe we are all soulmates at some level, I'm not going to write she's my soulmate and I'm glad we found each other. She is, however, the love of my life and the number one inspiration behind anything I do, which includes getting out of bed in the morning. Our 3 children have been challenging treasures throughout their lives – ever changing, ever growing, always wonders each unto themselves.

I have been fortunate to have 5 siblings who have spent their lives communicating to me that they believed I was a special and unique person. Our parents, especially my mother, taught me to find the light in everyone. It is a life lesson that continues to sustain me to this day.

I have been blessed with lifelong friendships that now near fifty years in time but are immeasurable in the more valuable life energy they bring to me. That said, I have been fortunate enough to find a workplace that has never been a workplace at all – a school that has been another wellspring of friendship. All of this has added life energy to the light within.

On the practical level, the constant challenge and push from a talented editor, Nick Yeager, who shared my vision has been a main ingredient. I choose the word "ingredient" purposely. Whatever has been stirred inside of me has multiple makeup and composition – Nick's probing questions and push for clarity really is what made this a "collection." I appreciate Tom Kelly and Kammie French for their friendship and perspective –they read each poem with open minds and reacted without filter, which was so necessary a step for one as insecure as I am. Elizabeth Zwolski's artwork is beyond amazing – I will be hard pressed to understand how she came to this vision; her talent is just so obvious and I am so very proud to have her work be part of this endeavor. In a practical sense, Brendan Leetch's understanding of fonts and print size and uploads and all the other words I do not understand became essential in putting this together.

In life one is fortunate if he or she has anyone to call inspiration. I have been guided by the wisdom of Dr. William Levin, Ph.D., in my practice as a counselor and in my life. My spirit has been fed and fostered by my spiritual mentor and guru, Louis Isert. Through them I found self-worth. Because of them I have been able to see what all those above have seen my whole life – a light within.

CHAPTER 13

The tube down his throat was the worst of them
   It was the one that would wake him with his slightest movement
   As he slept if he slept when he dreamt if he dreamt
He didn't know the difference any more.
The beeps and buzzers from the various machines around the bed didn't bother him
   He didn't understand what they were for and couldn't hear them anyway
   And could barely see them
                        If and when he bothered to look.

When he had a clear thought he wondered about the cost
   Being a Depression kid will do that to anyone, even now when it really matters
Very little.
He knew the grandsons helped move the old bed out
   And help the hospice people move the new bed in
   And then they all stood watch
   And he lived the nightmare he always swore he would never allow.
All the schedules changing, plans being made, will being checked and rechecked
   And the thousands of whispers, always whispers
Which made him secretly smile because he couldn't hear them if they were talking anyway.

The total body numbness made him thirsty
His gnarled hands were useless
He hadn't felt his toes in days
He didn't know if he was hungry
But ice chips helped

He tried to think of Josie
   Remember her smile
   Think of the way she would look at the kids with such pride and love
   Think of the way she watched the grandkids with such awe and joy
   Think of the way she tackled the laundry and kitchen with total determination
And how the cancer ate her until she begged to go

And yet...at the end, after all that unspeakable horror day after day after day
She bolted upright in bed and screamed, "Yes! Yes! Yes I come now!"
   And passed away with a smile on her discolored face.

Then it started.

It was all there in pieces
Flipping street cars, pitching pennies, playing pinochle, stealing potatoes, carrying
mattresses from one three flat to another, boot camp, the Canal,
Iwo, the bodies, the smell, Josie, the kids, two jobs, two houses, vacations,

1

little league, walking daughters down the aisle, burying parents and friends and...Josie

Just pieces and parts of pieces flying by and then and then...a light.

Is that it?

Is that the Light?

I was so scared, I am so scared, the pieces, I tried, do you see I tried, look at the pieces, I did my best

It's brighter, brighter, it's brilliant   it's perfect. it's here.

The pieces have disappeared.

PART I

It is revealed through individuals in the way they live life.

"I work here.   I am sad
                and genuinely happy
                and overwhelmingly proud
                and edge-of-my-seat excited
                and yes, it's possible
to feel all of them in the same moment, and it's ok, too."

NEIGHBOR

As he walked his shopping cart through the winter cold
   He rarely noticed the tune he whistled
   Some old Dionne Warwick song that wasn't about the way to San Jose
He never made it there, but cold nights like tonight he wished he had.
Tonight would be a good night for the alley behind the row of restaurants
   The ones the folks from the suburbs came in to use
      Or the folks from the high rises near the lake a few blocks away
The blowers would be on all night
   And that air was warm
   And he could hide his cart and curl near the dumpster
   And he could feel the blowers almost
   And with a blanket he could almost be warm

The walk was rough on the old streets and he kept forgetting to fix the spinning, rickety back left wheel on the cart
   So he had to stop every so often and make sure nothing fell out of the cart
   After a bump
It wasn't his whistling he heard which was why he heard it
   It was someone else's walking toward him, past him
      Toward the row of cars that was parked kiddie corner from the restaurant
     So they didn't have to pay to park
     Or tip a valet   which made him smile and shake his head
The new SUV sped past him like a shot
   So fast he stopped to watch
   And the whistling man never saw it
as he neared his car with his keys out in a hurry because he was without a coat
The car hit him so hard he flew like a bird, soared really, then spun like a top
   Then landed spread eagled on the street motionless facing the moon
     Like on a beach in the summer

The SUV raced away and no one came.
His first thought was help! help! help! in a group but one thought
He raced his cart back to the man and knew it was bad well before he got to him.
Speak to me say something oh my God this is bad I have to do something
Wait! Where's his phone? There it is he had it out in his hand.
9-1-1. 9-1-1. 9-1-1. Nothing. It was broken from the fall.
Two folks approached from the row of restaurants toward their car
   Cold in a hurry, man and woman
This man needs help this man needs help this man needs help
   Just get in the car honey, it's better if you don't look at them in the eyes.
Please help he got hit do something he needs help can you see he's alive but
   What did he do to him George? It doesn't matter close your door
They were gone.

4

Then another man in a jog, trying to look away
Please, sir, he's hurt, please do something, please call 9-1-1
The man looked into his eyes with   fear
    I can't be involved in this and sped away.

The hospital. 2 blocks. Behind the restaurant street. I need to get him in the cart
    The cart is full it's all I have it's all my stuff I got no other things without
my blanket Ill freeze and I need my hammer and my screwdriver and my
hats and bottles and all my other stuff
I have to get him into the cart
                              Dumping the cart at the curb where a car was parked
moments ago.
Searching through the pile and finding a postcard and putting it into his
coat
Picking up the broken body and laying it across the cart like an extra large
bag of dog food.
Running.
Another couple walking by
Running. Please help, call someone
Pushing, running, pushing, running

Emergency room entrance ahead
    A cold wind hitting him in the face, out of breath, no one around
A last deep breath
    Sprinting and pushing the cart right through the automatic doors
This man is alive and needs help!
What the hell who are you who is he you animal what have you done call
the police how did you get him into this thing my God he's got broken
bones get him in room 3 stat

Sitting on a ledge outside the emergency room
    Interviews over, wallet found, family notified, family arriving
    Multiple fractures, contusions, concussion...life. You can go now
The officer said quietly. He's going to make it.
My stuff is gone.
My Eagle cart is gone.
My blankets and extra hats are gone.
He reaches into his coat and takes out the post card.
    It's from someone to another someone   he knows neither
But it's from Pompano Beach
    Momma took him there once when he was little
    He looked at the picture and remembered the beach like it was
    He found that postcard one day and remembered and it made him smile
So he kept it.
He looked at it tonight and smiled, too.

2 CENTS

2 Cents.
    Not a whole lot
    But a whole lot on Christmas Eve, 1962
    To a seven-year-old when he can get that much for a Pepsi bottle
        When he returns it to a liquor store
        With a prominent display of penny candy at the cash register.
 2 Cents.
    When you're 4th of 6
    And the size runt of the 5 boy litter
    It's a nickname that has to do with chatter (and not amounts)
    When it's the only weapon in a near empty arsenal.
2 Cents.
    Always ready always shared always offered
        Even when uninvited.

Dear Santa I'm gonna prove you don't exist
    But just in case I want the new table top hockey game
    That has the removable metal men
    From all 6 original teams (I know all their names)
    And I want it to be mine
So they can be the Bruins or the Leafs or the Canadiens
    And I always get to be the Hawks.

2 Cents.
    I'm gonna go to bed after dinner like always on this night
        But fake like I'm sleeping
        So I can hear them
        And know before they come and get us
It was always them.
2 Cents.
    Dinner time Patriarchal Dad edicts
    "We're going to your Grandma's after dinner
    To celebrate my side tonight instead of next week..."
No we're not!
    It flew out was that out loud I kind of just thought it the plan the plan
the plan
    "You keep your mouth shut and do what you're told, fella."

Big Ford running all 8 in
    I forgot my purse   Sonofabitch!
    I need my cigarettes   Jesus H. Christ!
    I'll be right back   Hurry!
Moments or minutes but hours to a seven-year-old with a plan
                Johnny watch the kids while I help her find it
More moments and minutes...
                Donald watch the kids so I can help those 2
find it
They return bickering like always

Leading to a 3 hour party at Grandma's

2 Cents.
    The plan is in trouble
    How can I stay awake?
    When are we going home?
    I can't fake sleep unless I'm in bed expected to be asleep

Finally

    Up the steps behind a too slow Mom carrying a 1 year old sleeping sister
    Key in the lock
I'll restart the plan
    Under her arm (to get to the back of the house and into the bed)
But
    Inside the door
    Directly in front of him on the cocktail table
        A table top hockey game
Hawks vs. Red Wings
    Amidst a room full of toys
"Look who was here while we were gone."
    She says, baby in one arm

And purse in the other
    Holding 2 cents for at least another year.

APOSTLE

I

Brian hated therapy
    Just another feeling you haven't explored
You hate your Mom? You hate your Dad?
    You'd feel something like hate if they tied you up like they've tied me up
ADHD, ADD, GAD, mild to moderate depression   PILLS   lots of them
"We just have to get the combination right, then you'll feel ok."
    Said the doctor more than a half dozen times
Yeah, well, until then, Doc?   Go to therapy for me   tell him how I feel
now
Rage. Nothing makes it go away when it comes and he can't tell it's coming.
    When he's with Laura, there never is rage.   Peace. Calm. Acceptance.
        Is this what love is?   Attraction, infatuation   she listens   to me.

II

Saturday night   her house   parents out   no one home   but them
    She lives in a town called Unincorporated   her Dad's joke   he smiled
        Middle of nowhere   11 miles from his house   middle of somewhere

7

If it's love let's move to the next step   I don't do the next step
I love you   I love you
I want you   I want you
You turn me on   you turn me on
Then why?   I'm not doing that with anyone right
                                        now.
Please?   No.
You don't love me.   Yes I do.
Prove it.   That's sex, not proof.
DAMN IT!   Rage.   Again, but the first time with her   as he threw a chair
Then screw it then! He stormed out   Where are you going?
What do you care? No one cares! I don't care! What's the point? I'm done!
                              With us?   Like a little bird
With all of it everything he was out the door and in his van and down the
drive
     Screeching tires, speeding away

III

Stop sign two miles away way home at a 'T' no one around forest preserve
     To the right for miles
OhmyGod, why me?   AAAAAAAAAAGH!
     Floors it 50 60 70 80   hard turn right into the woods   van on two
wheels
     Airborne   ejected shot like a bullet   van tumbling
into trees
     Lying in bushes   waking up blood in mouth hands ears all over
How am I alive?
     Knees push grab a bush feet stumble almost fall fall repeat
     Up steady dark path his body made car ahead lights slowly by   hey
Can't yell pain is now real skull badly bleeding, torn, flapped over, get to
the road
Stumbling on the road no one no one no one
     1 am bleeding worse get back to Laura's how? Two miles, not enough
blood
                    Inside of me   dizzy
Huh? At the stop sign   a car   huh?   Old car, beat up Chevy, stickers all
over

IV

He didn't know
     Laura called his parents   her parents   911
She left and slowly tried to follow his known path   passed him in the
woods
                    Didn't see him
His parents left home following the same path
Police, rescue, dispatched

8

V

Dude, you're hurt. Need a ride?
    In the car   long hair, hippie?, army shirt, beard, moustache
             Back seat a commercial for fast food everywhere empty wrappers
You're bleeding bad. Hospital?
   No. Laura's. Please Laura's.
Where does Laura live?
   Back that way.
     Car turning around fast
Hold the top of your scalp down tight. Breathe slow. What's your name?
   Brian.
Hi, Brian. I'm Peter.
   Where did you come from?
Back that way. Is this the turn?
   Yes.
Hold that tight, man. Stay with me.
     Car stopped on Laura's lawn   Peter carries him to the porch   out

VI

Sirens
   Parents EMTs police Laura's parents
     Laura, holding his hand in the back of the ambulance
We found the van   two miles away on 120 in the forest preserve
   Two miles? How did he get here?   Son? How did you get on the porch?
Peter. It was Peter. He picked me up in his old Chevy
   Peter who?
The hippie guy in the beat up Chevy. He drove me here
   What hippie? What Chevy?
He carried me up to the porch   Laura? Did you see Peter?
     Hand squeezed. Tight.
   We found you here on the porch   your Mom and me and the
ambulance
   Pulled up at the same time   there was no hippie. there was no
Chevy.
Yes there was.   And he squeezed back tightly.

BEGGAR

The army jacket is faded green
Like he could've gotten it at the thrift store
Or a church giveaway on a PADS night.
But
If he thought about it (and he didn't)
He would remember he was issued the jacket
The same day he got those great boots
That he traded for a fix under the viaduct on Vincennes 2 winters ago. (It

9

was cold, he should've held out for 2.)

He lays there, barely awake, mumbling
In case someone listens, so he can recite what's on the cardboard
That's now barely readable on the ground by his side

"Vet, out of work, homeless, please help."

Might've been last Wednesday the last time he said the whole sentence.
But the cold puts strangers' hands into his extra large McDonald's coffee
cup
With change
And the occasional dollar

On weekdays when he's awake he can sometimes get 30-40 dollars
But he's not awake much and when he is he's high
Or in Da Nang

Those days are the worst days, the Da Nang days
Because the folks in their suits
And their dresses and hats
Look like Cong, they're Cong
And their chatter makes no sense
And it's Cong chatter
And he holds his M-16 straight and fires
Even yells bang-bang when he does
And no one falls they keep walking
And chattering
And some laugh
(and it's the only time anyone looks directly at him)

And so he runs and runs and cries
'cause Tommy got blowed up and Johnny's gut shot
And he's sure he saw Little Alvis' head rolling in that alley
These Cong are vicious and he runs and runs and
He finally gets under the train bridge
And the man takes his McDonald's cup and empties it
And a guy from a church gives him a clean needle
And he sits up against the wall with a tied up arm
And is back in Da Nang again
But it's ok now
Like it was the first time
And Little Alvis' head disappears

And he drools and smiles and yells, "I did it for y'all!"
But no one understands him who can hear him
(anyway)

10

CARDBOARD MAN

I

The little boy in the park
   Told his Mommy
   "Look there's the cardboard box man!"
When he stood in the box   startling them as they walked by
   His smile was wide and mostly toothless

He always smiled when he heard that
   always heard it
   always when he stood in the box
when awakened from the noise of passers-by.

Hear that Momma?
You said I never amount to nothin
You was wrong
I'm cardboard man and that's not nothin!

II

She yelled
            mostly at him, about him
Said he was more hassle than he was worth
Said he even cost more than his check
Said she was never gonna pay for the extra work
    He needed 'cause he told a teacher he saw the letters ok but they
was backward
    'cause teacher kept yelling at him to read the simple word on the card
         she put on his desk
('sides he could read what he needed to
       signs: STOP, OPEN, MENS, FREE, BUY ONE GET ONE FREE)

Teacher just kept yellin
Extra lady kept yellin
Momma kept yellin   extra lady stopped comin
So
He stopped going   no one ever came to see him or why
'cept the men to see Momma
Mostly she made him stay in the closet   and promise not to watch
   And listen to her scream (but not like yellin) their names
Freddie and Tommie and Johnny and Derek
Tony and Richard and Kelvyn and Myron
   He memorized them all
   In the correct order
   Just in case one might be his Daddy but
Nobody ever was.

III

One day he came out
    Only 'cause he really had to pee
    And the last time he peed in the closet he really got a whoopin
But Lamar stopped and Momma said don't mind him but Lamar got up and
left
And Momma shook her head and said you ain't never gonna be no good
and now I didn't get my money   (but no whoopin)

Then she went out for cigarettes and never came back.

The landlord said you ain't got no rent you gotta get out
But he didn't understand him until the policeman said it, too.
    It was cold on the park bench   the policeman said you can't sleep here
So he walked to another park   different policeman same thing
So he walked to the church, which he hated going to
    ('cause them alleluias and amens and singin and praisin he never could
understand)
But the pews were better than the park bench and it was warm and the preacher
let him stay but said it was not forever.

IV

When the preacher made him go
    The church was getting new furniture   the boxes were big and cardboard
and in the alley and no one said no you can't so he took the
biggest one
And went back to the park, but in the woods, where the police never go
It took time, but he found out
                  From a bus driver about a soup kitchen
              From a man by the barber shop about public bathrooms
              From the soup kitchen lady about another soup kitchen
for different days
              From the preacher there about the shelters
Which he would visit but not stay
    'cause he could eat and wash there
    And get his teeth brushed
    And change up his clothes sometimes   in the winter get gloves and stocking
cap
    And get his pair of warm boots ('cause the sign said FREE and he could
read it)

But always, every night, back to the park, back to the woods, back to his
box
    It was his
    And Momma was wrong

'cause he was somebody.

CART BOY

The part time job was a godsend
   Gas money, insurance money, spending money
     "You're going to be in college in a year, you need a job."
Two days a week, 4-9, either weekend day, all day, 17 hours, give or take.

Stand at the end of the line, checker is the boss, bag.
   Bread on top.   Cans on the bottom.   Frozen special plastic wrapper.
    Fill the cart   gently.   Cases of water or soda on the bottom.
      Smile. Be courteous. Thank you for coming, do you need help?

Last one there   cart duty.   Rain, sleet, snow, heat   get the carts
   From the cart corral to the store   push together   line them up
    Cart in the far corner in the Wendy's lot   go get it   get them all
       Don't be the last one there.

Band practice   4 times a week   twice the drum line has to stay after
   Always the days work starts at 4   flying into the lot, punching in at 3:57
       or 3:58

"You were here last, Tim. You're the cart boy today."   Every day.
   Nickname.   "Afternoon, cart boy."   Laughter.
On crowded Saturdays he could get 75 going at once
   "What are you doing? You can't move 50 carts at once!"
     (I've done 78, but you don't know that, sir.)   Yes, sir. Sorry, sir.
   "It's rainy, so what? You're gonna get wet anyway."
     Right, sir.

98 degrees.   Carts everywhere.   Old couple parks way too far from the
store.
   Why do they want to walk so far?   Why do they always wear long
sleeves?
    "Would you like some help to your car, Ma'am?"
    "No. We're fine. You aren't getting a tip out of us."
    "We can't take tips from customers, sir, I just wanted to offer
assistance."
    "Sure you did."   Cough. Sweat well below the armpits.   "Hah!"

It seemed like only seconds later   where is that voice coming from?
Across the lot   the old folks   the lady who didn't speak   "Help!"
Running. Hot. Sprinting. Her voice meek, but louder as he approached.
"Help!"
   He was blue.   On the ground behind the open trunk.   Mouth wide
open.

"Ma'am, call 911!"
   "Help!"
"Ma'am, please call 911!"
   "Help!" She stood frozen in place, staring at the blue face on the parking

lot.

Phone in hand, 911, send, shirt off, behind his head
    "911, what is your emergency?"

Counting to 30, 2 breaths, counting to 30, 2 breaths, counting to 30, 2
breaths
    "Help!" Over and over, frozen in the blazing heat.   Sirens
Counting to 30. 2 breaths, counting to 30, 2 breaths.   Lights and noise
"Son, how many times have you?"
"5."
"Perfect."
A cough, from far away, and another, and he's turned, and vomit, and
EMTs.
    A board and oxygen and machines and speed   and a pulse
        EMT helping her   the rest with him   carting him onto the
ambulance

Boss just appears it seems   standing right next to him
    "Ok, Tim, looks like the excitement is over."
EMT   "I know you're the manager, but do you know what this boy just
did?"
    "Sure. He called 911."
        "Yes. While he administered CPR.
            And brought this man back.
            And saved his life."
    "Really? He's just a cart boy."

But Tim didn't hear him.
    He spied two carts near the Wendy's drive-through
        He had to make sure to get them
            Before a car hit one, and there would be hell to pay.

DEAR SANTA

At Jerry's retirement party, his then former colleagues reveled in his approaching
    unbusyness.
They toasted his patience, his dedication, his even temperament, his acceptance of
everyone, his sense of humor, his love of life
Claire did, too, and thought about Sundays of rest
    with no more tension as Monday and the work week loomed larger as
the night wore on
    with conversation instead of silence
    with restful sleep instead of tossing and turning and pacing and garbled angry
speech if there was any real sleep at all

he just tinkered around the house
    fixing the drip on the basement faucet
    fixing the crack on the garage gutter

14

fixing the lathe on the screen door in the back
rewiring his living room with the neighbor so Claire could have Surroundsound
    with the new flatscreen he received as a retirement gift
    that he hung on the wall across from her favorite chair

He just seemed so happy to be doing nothing (of substance, anyway)
    Which is why she was surprised when he told her that he interviewed
    For a part time job
    At the mall, after Thanksgiving
Before she could object, he told her it was seasonal, and he would be done
with it before Christmas.

His first day of work was Black Friday
    He had to be there at 4 a.m.
    He went into the bathroom to get ready at 2:30
    And didn't come out until 3:45   dressed as Santa Claus.
She wanted to laugh, she wanted to call the kids, she wanted to ask him
what in God's name was he thinking   but she just stared as he kissed her
and said he'd be home after work
just like he had done for 40 years at the   plant

Always loving Christmas came in handy to Jerry that season
As did the idea of gluing on the beard
As did the extra twenty pounds he had gained since his right knee was
scoped
    and he and Claire didn't walk around the lake any more.
As did his patience, and even-temperament, and sense of humor

Getting crying 2 year-olds to smile was a test
    And the money was made in the pictures
Actually being interested in the newest video game every boy wanted
    And pretending to know how it worked, and how to win at it
While balancing a 3rd child on his swollen knees
And almost begging the little girl named Lisa to quit pulling the beard
While comforting the embarrassed couple after their little Shaun puked
everywhere
    While figuring a way to make the North Pole sound mystical and exciting
for the 500th time
    While explaining that Rudolph is great, but he loves all the reindeer
    While holding the more than a dozen children who were lost and
keeping them from crying until their parents were found

All the way to his last shift, 15 minutes before he punched out for the last
time
    A little boy named Logan sat on his lap
    The last in line
    Dad 2 feet away, boy staring in tears, terrified
    "What can Santa bring you for Christmas?"
    "I want my Mommy to come home" as Dad cried nearby.

"Well, so do I, Logan. But Santa can't bring people. But I promise to come to your house, ok?"
As Dad nodded in tears and Logan said yes and thanks and hugged him tightly.

As Jerry drove away from the mall
   he figured he'd be back next year
life could be busy   and the mall could use the seasonal help

EGGS AND OPERA

Part of the morning routine
  Was the throat spray after brushing his teeth
   And gargling with a generic Listerine
               Which he got two for one at Walgreens.

He would recite Bomarzo word for word
   on the bike on his way
   to the back door
   that led him into the kitchen.

As he hung up his coat
And fired up the grill
He began to hum the first scene

Making sure the pans were clean
Rescrubbing his flippers
Using steel wool on the cooking fork
   That kind of physical work required humming only
   As if he were in the orchestra pit
              Warming up.

The town workers orders were always up before six
             before it was light
             before he felt his voice was ready
Yet there they were…

He could belt out the baritone, but here he sang the part softly
He could fake the tenor pretty well, so softly was good, so he didn't hear his mistakes…
Alto, soprano he just whistled (to a crescendo when tossing two eggs into the air)
By the end of the morning rush
  He could get through the entire opera
  And at least three encores…
And this morning as Marita grabbed the last two plates
  Pushing the door from the kitchen to the tables in one motion with her hip

16

He could hear the voices of an appreciative audience
    As they marveled at the creations on their plates
    Bill the plow driver, big burly, and loud...
    "Now, Marita, that omelet is a work of art."

In the kitchen he silently bowed
    imagined the bouquets being tossed nearby...
    For another performance done well.

HOSPICE LADY

I felt you just moments ago
    I don't mean actually touching you
    Like 90 minutes ago when I bumped your side
                while I checked your blood pressure
                and your heart rate
                and your breaths per minute
On the machines that measure the precious moments you have left.

I felt you when you leaned so slightly
    With all your strength
    Achingly forward
    So you could hear the voices of your 6 grown children in the corner of the
kitchen next door.

Just so you know
    I went and told them to move closer to the door so you could hear
better
And they were just so smug and smart
And telling me you couldn't hear them anyway
    you did nothing but moan and groan for almost a year
    the dementia was advanced
    you couldn't recognize a person, a picture, or even yourself in a mirror
even if you wanted and they wanted and the prayers were done and they
were all ok with it.

Like they know.

They gave me their terms ("It's not really Alzheimer's but a dementia just
like it")
        and their medical descriptions (plaque at critical points; synapses
misfiring)
        and their behavioral reports (at the end he just stared straight
ahead)
as if you were in there, up there, inside the massive skull that holds your empty
eyes

So I smiled and told them to move because I didn't really care about none
of that
                              because it didn't matter
                              because I've been doing this a long time
and I know you can hear them plain as day
and they moved out of respect
                         for me
                         or for you
                         or for things they don't understand.

I felt you because I know you're still here
And I feel you now
Especially since they said good night and went their separate ways
And I knew you were waiting for them to go
                         So they wouldn't be here when you made your final move.
(like at school when I learned all about the machines
                         And how they measure
                         And what they measure)
And how Doreen pulled me aside and said know that for sure but always
know there ain't no machine that tells you what you really need to know in this
work

And I know you're there because she was right and I can always feel it
Ever since.
And now I know you're ready
And I'm smiling for you and we both know how they're all such fools
Because they think you're finished
But I feel you there
And I feel your impatience
And I know you're ready
And I know you're moving on

There you go; I feel you leaving
Go in peace.

Funny how those machines are always about 30 seconds behind
I'll go shake your boy and tell him
My work is done.

Godspeed.

MAILMAN

Sorting letters sorting letters sorting letters
     The machines can do a lot of crazy things at a hundred miles an hour
     But some things you still need a person for
Sorting letters.

18

Mostly these days it's monthly advertising magazines
And brochures
And half off coupons
That need to be cut out with scissors
J. Crew, J.C. Penney, Crestfield Mall, Buffalo Wild Wings, Victoria Secret
And on and on and on
Made the bag heavier   and more monotonous.
He was running about ten minutes late all morning
Back up in the McDonalds coffee line's what started it
Supervisor standing in silence over their shoulders for twenty straight minutes
Made it a sure thing he would never make his rounds on time
And the government would get another fifteen or twenty minutes free,
on him.

Most of the new rules made no sense to him
He just knew they tossed round words like "Billions of dollars in debt"
Like it was just a handful of quarters that could bring down an institution
Which at one time was the pride of the western world

He fired up the jeep
And smelled deeply to make sure the FreshWave took the cigar scent
out
Like Bill Miller told him it would at Hank's tavern
After bowling last week
"Maybe if we didn't spend millions on a fleet of jeeps that break down a
lot"
(his was in great shape 'cause he worked on it back in the garage on his
own time)
"maybe if we found people who cared enough to walk
And get to know their route
And the people on their route"
Like he used to back in the days when he knew the names of everyone in
the office, which he didn't any more

Windy and warm.
Good, 'cause the cigar smoke would be out of the jeep before it was ever
in.
Good, 'cause he wouldn't sit in sweat on the leather seat and turn the light
blue shirt into dark blue mush
Good, 'cause the wind would blow in his face on 45 and Midlothian and any busy
road where he could bump it over 40.

Cursing the no outlets because the streets were winding
And everyone had to be creative
When it took putting in a new mailbox
Not many standard issues in those blocks with the never ending cul-de-sacs with
No way out except turning around

Checking under his seat
The new bag of extra large IAMS power snacks just over half full

Mrs. Mulvaney's box   ads need a rubber band to hold them all together
And he gently laid the large bone atop the pile

That pooch Charlie (who names a dog Charlie, even if it is a mutt?)
is cute   this treat will give him the energy to be out here on a hot day.

USHER

The alarm sounded at 6:15 sharp
    Sunday was the only day he used the alarm clock
So it startled him, like it did each week
Up until 2 years ago, 6:30 worked just fine, but the two block walk took him longer
as did the routine of getting ready.
He didn't remember when he awoke when Annie was alive, because she
never needed an alarm clock
    And she would always shake him when she got out of the shower.

He had the shower water extra hot
    As it was most days, because it took a bit more to get the night's chill out
He had always hated being cold,
He smiled at that irony while standing in the steaming stream
    Born, raised, married, and raising a family in Chicago
    While constantly (it seemed, anyway), fighting the cold and chill.

Into the bedroom in front of the mirror
    Clothes freshly pressed
    Allowing himself another smile of pride
    Still doing his own ironing at 86
    A Saturday afternoon or evening ritual to look his best for 7:30 Mass
On Sunday morning.

Always a white shirt and black pants, with a black tie that he tied to reach
his waist
These details were important, ritual is ritual
Cuff links and usher badge, top right drawer like always
(Where Annie kept them, it was a good idea)
The same cuff links, 101st Airborne, a gift from a D-Day reunion in 1969
Badge up the right sleeve after the sport coat

Today he wouldn't need the overcoat
    Mornings were cool in April but it was still unseasonably warm
The two block walk took over twenty minutes now
    He was often offered rides, even the kids wanted to come in and drive
him
He wouldn't have it.
The neighborhood had changed, they were worried
But it was 7:15 on Sunday morning, and he was an 86 year-old man
With an usher badge on his sleeve.

The crowd at the 7:30 Mass was small
    And over the last year shrunk even more
But he still believed what he was doing was an important task
    Even though if Benny Biondo was sick again
He would usher alone   and perhaps, no one would even notice.
He remembered when it was crowded and he actually showed folks to
open seats
And he remembered when it was necessary that he go pew by pew at Communion
to keep order.

He said hello to Fr. O'Rourke, Pastor Emeritus, and was glad
    He was saying Mass
    He appreciated ritual
    He remembered when it was crowded
    His homilies were never longer than 7 minutes.

He lit the two candles he always lit
    Put the $2 in the box
    Knelt on the kneeler and prayed
For Murph and for Annie and their souls.
He slept with Annie for 63 years of marriage
    And held her as she died in their bed
He slept in a tent or foxhole with Murph for 6 months
    And held him as he died in the Ardennes forest

He offered the Mass itself for the kids
And the grandkids and the great grandkids like always
But as he left the church
    He stole a glance back to the rack of candles
    And blew a kiss to Annie and Murph
    And tugged his cuff links and softly touched his badge.

OLD NUN

As she held her elbow up against the massive door jamb
And rested with rapid breaths,
She dipped her other hand in the font full of water and automatically
crossed herself with her fingers   on a hand that was already wet
From the sweat of the walk
From the convent to the church.

She made her way to the front pew of the church and began the process of
genuflection
And knew, it, too, was automatic, and only age made the action a process.

She was proud to be on the kneeler in the dark, dusky, cold church
Of the 7 elderly nuns left in the convent, she was the only one who even attempted
to make it to the church

The rest happy with Father stopping by with Communion and daily prayers,
And the occasional Mass
Although this new Fr. Martinez from the South had dispensed with
formalities
As soon as he had taken the reins of the aching, dying parish
And the nuns couldn't work in the behemoth school that was one quarter
filled with students whose families couldn't pay one quarter the tuition necessary
"There can be no more daily Mass in the convent, Sisters. It's a manpower issue
more than anything else"

She wrapped the Rosary around her left hand as she had done each
morning for 68 years
(it had been 3 years since she had finished saying an actual Rosary – since
she started to lose her place and the beads began to confuse her)
The Rosary itself gave her a secure feeling that she still had command

"You do that again, Johnny Riordan, and you'll get the pointer on your backside"
"First row, get your coats. Second row, check your desks. Third row, pens
and pencils away"
"Look at McGrath, just sitting there, all the brains in the world, choosing to
use them for a seat cushion. Sure McGrath, let someone else come up with answer.
Is Leslie Murphy going to be there every time you need an
answer?"
"I don't care if your father OWNED the bar, Clancy. He was in the bar; you
were supposed to be at church, at confession. Now you have to go two
weeks in a row!"
"If you want to read, Miss Milton, take out your reader. The class is singing. That is
a music book you're holding. Sing!"

She looked around. Everyone stood but her.
It was already the Gospel and she was lost again, in thoughts, and moments and
classes and students

"If you can't go into the bathroom without making a ruckus, then you can't
go into the bathroom. Understand, Healy?"
"You can clap erasers after school until 6th grade for all I care, Mr. Hayden.
But I'll get that smirk off your face. Or you will"
"There are 26 letters in the English alphabet, Miss Mangan. Your 'q's and
'g's are identical. No student of mine is inventing a new alphabet with 25 letters.
Practice!"

"Sister Demetria, the Body of Christ"
She looked around and realized she was in the Communion line.
Fr. Martinez went to place the Host in her hand.
Her tongue defiantly leapt out of her throat. His groan was audible as she
mumbled "Amen" without letting the Host get near a tooth.

"Yes, you're promoted to 5th grade, Wilson. I need the desk."
"You cross your thumbs when you fold those hands, Miss Moriarty, so you
remember why you're here"

"You write that prayer 10 times perfectly and you'll always remember it perfectly when you need it"
The Church was empty.
The half a block back would seem longer today.
The cane wasn't much of a help any more.
She splashed the water on her forehead as she crossed herself. 300 days indulgence is 300 days indulgence.
Maybe Fr. Martinez needs to learn a thing or two about history and legacy and ritual.
She had to try and remember to offer up Mass for him   tomorrow.

PRIEST

"Go in peace."
He said it automatically, robotically, in monotone
    Like so many of the other times
                        Out of the over 8000 times
He had said it.
 They answered, all 17 of them, and he didn't hear their thanks or the be or the to
        Or the 'G' word

He was in the sacristy in moments, and had hung up the vestments
    And it was all in a fog, as if he were a witness in a trial and would be
        Hard pressed to relate all he had done as truth
            Because it was all so same so ritual so empty so   much   air.

He walked to check the doors of the church after the last one left, after the last candle was lit after the last quarter was put in the poor box (it used to be a dollar to light a candle, not any more).
    There was ice in the corner in the crack in the marble by the St. Joseph statue
        It was cold in there
                    But it was over 40 April why this ice
        The building over 100 years old had seen its share of ice
                    But now on the inside
        The carpeting in the left trancept was threadbare
                There was gum caked under the pews in the back opposite the
Virgin
        And last week he noticed a gang symbol carved into front right pew 10
As he locked the doors he remembered when they could be always open
    And when a nun wouldn't get punched and robbed in the convent walkway
        And when every pew had at least a few bodies in it for each Mass
        And when the collections were in the thousands, not hundreds

Maybe that's when doubt slithered in like the snake it is.

He fought the fight and lived the cliché

Senseless murders and lavish funerals
Unwanted pregnancies mothers and children disappearing
("forgive me father," "forgive him father," "forgive us father")
Numbers down, closing the school, diocese pressure, roofing bills,
cleaning bills, energy bills, tax bills (not all church matters are untaxed, who
knew?)
In three years a baby in the same bathroom in a towel in a blanket in a
shirt
Homeless sleeping in pews   how did they get in   better locks, father

Walking in the brisk morning across the courtyard to the rectory
The spring's first dandelion right in the middle of the lawn
He frowned and shrugged and remembered that lawn was
immaculate
When they could pay janitors and he had the time
Or the retired older parishioners volunteered and kept it
Immaculate
But he had buried the last of them years ago.

He ate burnt toast and drank black coffee and thought about the snake
And how his prayers would echo in the empty rectory
And the sound would sprinkle to the ground like ice crystals
Falling from the roof that needs work

I speak because I have to I am supposed to I was trained to I always did so I
do

I thought I used to see
I believed in signs
I was sure there was presence and I felt lucky
To be chosen to notice. Then the snake. Slithering.

Another night at the funeral parlor
"eternal rest grant unto him..." and tears and hugs and thanks for
coming
To gather snippets to make a funeral homily make sense to anyone still listening
Turning the corner to the rectory
She's lying on the curb, screaming
Young man standing over her   she looks to be grabbing her bag
Left hand on her shoulder   crawling away from him, away
from him
Holding her down firmly   swinging and flailing arms and legs
Out of the car in slow motion   stop a felony   is that what I'm called to do
The young man's voice, firm, yet soft
"It's ok, Ma'am, you fell, it will be ok. I have you. I've called for help."
His other hand holding a cell phone
Ambulance, police, reports, and a thank you
"She just needed help, Father."
"But you chose to give her some, son."
"You would've done the same thing."

"Perhaps."

A walk across the dark courtyard, a pause.

Night prayers said at his desk
                    Like always
        But with purpose and passion missing for months.
        Lights out, pillow fluffed, blanket pulled back
                    Like always
and then a sudden
drop to his knees
    used to pray from his knees   used to pray from his knees   used to
Used to when it mattered and he was humble and he believed

            Tears   not cried in years

"Please, please, please. I am so sorry.
                    Just keep showing me the dandelions –
And I promise
                    I will never miss the flowers

            again."

SNOW MAN

It was thick and sticking and slippery and already deep
    And it was only 3:30, and it took him 30 minutes to make the 10 minute trip
                From school to home (even with 4 wheel drive).

He loaded his ski gear in the SUV, this time remembering the thicker gloves
    (the Christmas pair from Uncle Joe were just too thin and wouldn't do)
He went back inside to change into the snow pants
    To save time when he got to the mountain
Mom's Jeep was blocking him in when he got back outside
"What are you doing?"
"Going skiing. Don't worry. I'll be careful on the roads. If I leave now I'll beat the rush hour traffic-"
"And the snow?"
"It's everywhere. And great. The mountain is calling me, Mom."
"Tom."
"Mom, I shoveled good enough. It's workable. I have to go now"
"And the O'Grady's?"
"Awww, c'mon, Mom. I need to leave now. If I do their driveway, I'll get to the mountain and have to turn around and come right back."
"You promised them."
"I won't be able to ski."
"You promised them"

The monologue in his head was unkind as he worked the long, sloping drive
   They never even go anywhere
   I haven't seen them since before Thanksgiving anyway
   How about hiring a plow? They gotta have some money.
   Why this big driveway anyway
   How do you spell retirement community?

He felt the tightness in his legs and back
   And it made him madder that it was similar to what Mike and Bill and Don
Were feeling on the mountain right now
   The snow was heavier now, and deeper
   Couldn't just push it across like his driveway
Almost done.
Near the end of the driveway.
Even nightmares end
   He could hear them all laughing and telling stories at lunch tomorrow
   He wanted to scream
        to swear
        to fling the shovel in the pile and just walk next door and lie on the
couch.

The plow didn't mean it, because plows can't.

But a new, foot and a half pile was deposited along the end of the O'Grady
driveway, up to the mailbox.
   He would be another half hour.
   He screamed this time, no words, in a primal way.
   As he got to the last shovel-full, he looked in each direction
      Daring another plow to come along
Finished. A step toward home

"Tom?"
The voice faint, tired, old.
"Tom?"
Again.
He turned slowly, and there they stood, in their doorway
   Halfway in, halfway out
Mr. O'Grady waved him to them
   So he walked up, wondering what else needed to be done.

Mrs. O'Grady handed him a large cup of homemade hot chocolate
   With marshmallows
"I think I remember   this is how you like it, right?"
"Yes, Ma'am. Thanks."
"No, Tom. Thank you."

He looked at his lifelong neighbors
   The snow hit their faces already wet with tears.

RAIN MAN

Numbers were always his milieu
   A statement on a Mathematics award in high school
   (the vocabulary word reminding the English department he was theirs)
ACT 36 perfect score
   Suggesting academic excellence in all areas
   Yet he knew numbers; he knew his milieu
Even though he knew most everything anyone had presented to him.

The University wanted to show him off
   They created a new Calculus class
   Really just for him
That he helped teach by term's end.
He didn't like the extra attention
   He felt symposiums, high school nights, Math conferences
Were freak shows, and he was in a cage at a zoo
And he would smile, in a suit, behind a table, in a cage
   Signing occasional autographs made him feel like showering
He thought he wasn't an athlete or politician or scientist or TV personality
   He knew numbers   and people confused him.

The company that recruited him off the campus
   And hired him   was perfect.
Not too big, his own cubicle
   Books and books of numbers
   That needed work
Consistent correct legal neat orderly

The nickname came quickly
   He ate lunch at his desk
   He answered any question sincerely honestly correctly not unfriendly
But never asked one
   He didn't have any.

Somehow someone someday found out
   They all heard of Enron and bubbles and banks
   And Fannie Mae and foreclosures
But no one ever met anyone who knew all the numbers
And understood it all, chapter and verse, case by case.

At first they were uncomfortable
   Then he was just theirs
A sideshow, perhaps, but theirs
   And he always answered every question anytime
Correctly.

So someone in HR shared and they knew
   At break time on December 14
   He stepped out for a walk to the bathroom

27

(at 10:07, like every other day)

When he returned, the birthday cake was filled
   With lit candles
   One for each year
The singing was off key
   But he smiled and they smiled and he blew out the candles
There was an awkward moment of silence after applause
   But he said thanks
   Someone cut the cake
   He even got a piece
And they all went back to work.

He felt it was prudent not to mention
   That right away when the song began he noticed
The cake was one candle short.

SAX MAN

He was in a hurry
   Seemed like that's the way it always was and was always gonna be from
here on out
Metra station in Glenview, L platform in Ravenswood, southwest corner of Union
Station (when the right beat cops were there to pretend he wasn't),
then back

Sometimes all the way up to Lake Forest on Metra, but only when he felt it, 'cause
if he spent all that time goin' up there he had to make it worth it
He had to push it
He had to hurry
He had to play   and he had to be good.

He liked those days
         The ones he felt it
         Like the music was part of him and all he had to do was
let it out
         And the horn was like it was like it was like a part of him
An arm, a leg, a lung, an ear, the sax.
He would play and he could hear it and he would play and it was like he was
listening to a stereo on laundry duty when he did the deuce at Joliet

Which was why he was in a hurry 'cause he had to pay the rent
Never can be late
Never can be trouble
Never can have any outstanding bills
Or his P.O. would have him back and be squeezing him
And be wanting to know how he made all this cash
And was he back in the game

And was he back on the corner
And was he back with his boys

And he knew no P.O. was gonna believe he made the rent with a horn
And he was in a hurry so he could pay the rent
And then he could see Germaine on Friday just like Jessie promised
And he could have him til Sunday like last time

He made the rent and made it to Glenview before the big rush
And opened the sax case and laid it out in front of him
And sat like a snake charmer playing for a cobra
And began to play

And it was Glenview and when he played there he always thought of Mr.
Doory
'cause he was the white dude who taught him the most about the sax
And told him he had a gift
And told him to respect the sax
And told him to honor the music by always playing his best
No matter if it was at Chicago Theater (which he did, once)
Or the Glenview train platform
Or an alley near the Eisenhower
When Lil Johnny said play and play good and maybe I won't kill you for shorting
me on that coke

And Mr. Doory made him play all that white folk stuff when he wanted to
play Kool and the Gang
Mr. Doory said there would be time for that stuff later
(And he was right, 'cause Kool and the Gang saved him in Maywood that night)
But that white folk music paid the rent
And he smiled and thought it was funny how all that works out

And a man in a $300 suit threw a $10 bill in his case and said,
"Man, I have never heard 'Somewhere Over the Rainbow' played with such
elegance."
Elegance? Damn
He giggled just a bit and thought

That man don't know a thing about elegance

And started to play 'Moonlight Serenade' as a crowd gathered with their smiles
and wallets.

RUNNER

The right knee, full of arthritis, in a constant slightly swollen state
    Aleve and ice help (who really ices anymore?)
    Neoprene pad tightens it enough so the floating cartilage only
occasionally slams into the inflamed nerves around
The left knee, single lathe wrap on the bottom to ward off the right's
condition
For now.

The shelf life for both limited
30 years of couch and lazy boy and chair with ottoman and TV and
crosswords
And why walk when you can ride and why get up when you have kids and
why now when there is always later and why pretend it hurts it really hurts
Left calf tight, always ready to cramp
Tendonitis in the right arm how can that hurt while running but it does
Wart near the second toe on the bottom of the right foot can one run on a rock?

Over 50 pounds and two years
Wheezing on a street corner after hurrying to avoid a car
    After the change of light midway across a wide street
    "If you die I'm screwed" but not that nice

The first quarter mile always the same what the hell am I doing this sucks I can't I
feel everything all over and most of what I feel is unpleasant and
hurts
Then a turn, a pace, a wall gone through
Legs up and down arms not flailing any more
Watch check already a mile can I feel this good hill not bad head up feel...projected
smiling...that is somehow real.

Second mile third mile wandering mind pumping arms who am I mad at
what I would say this is how to say it maybe I'll do this hehehehehehe that went
well, yeah that will work it feels good to get that out there and just
say it

Fourth mile
        Euphoria
        Can't believe I can go this far at my age
        Floating
        Look where I am
Wow.
If the knees hurt, that's part of another experience
The feet are fine
There is no burning
Last week's cigars are back in mile two by the railroad tracks
Staccato breaths in four step rhythm
Works for me.

Past six miles, homeward bound
Last hill here just to remind me
                              I have conquered nothing
But today.

Arms pump, shorter steps, arms pump, hill gone
Turn toward home
An attempt at a sprint, no, a sprint, an actual sprint...
Staving off the inevitable in my own terms

while I still can.

BALL BOY

I

If the peppers were easiest
    The zucchini was hardest
        Moody, given to sudden blossom or failure
    The carrots never gave them trouble   once he built her the metal screen
And in a city garden   carrots are a luxury

She would fit it all in that yard
    Like it was a small farm near Naples   not a yard behind a bungalow
    Without a garage into the alley   on the southside of the city

He would come home from a ten hour shift
    She would be out there
        Hands and knees, gloves, scarf across her head
        Talking, singing, praising, cajoling   plants   as if they were children
    the doctors said they couldn't have any   the doctors said   the doctors said
    in serious tones in answer to "what if it's God's will?"   you can't have any
        as she cried late at night in the bathroom when he was in bed
        and she thought he was asleep
        but he wasn't   he lay and stare at a blank ceiling with no answers

So she worked the garden like it was a nursery.

II

It was after a long hard day of humid and rain and sweat
    He was out there to help dig   and he saw the footprints   more footprints
Ruined cabbage   more footprints and beans torn up too early
Hands and knees what happened spreading the leaves of the plants and there it
                        Was   a ball   a whiffle ball in the lima beans
He stood with the ball and looked into the yard and alley beyond
    Where the neighbor boys played their ball in game after game
    Storming toward the back fence to the alley

31

Yelling why   why   why   you ruined some beans   but in Italian
He didn't know English well enough to yell like he needed to
   Boys scattered and laughed and ran and laughed some more
   Turning toward the house, tripping and falling   over over over
         Another ball, this one a regulation league ball
More yelling, mostly in Italian with one line in English
         "If I ever get a ball you no see it ever again!"   He meant it.

III

When the cancer came it hit her like the freight train it was
   Long and full and in the way relentless and never ending
      She would sit in a sun hat on a lawn chair in the yard
         And coach him   pull this, replant that, snip that branch, dig dig dig
He would show her the asparagus, she'd smile and nod
         bring her two strawberries, she'd pretend to like them
         cut a carrot and wash it off and she'd chew it and smile
The balls would fly in
               And bounce in
                  And fly in
         She would beg him not to get upset so he'd just smile
And never once give a ball back   and snicker if they looked at him
                              nod when they swore at him
                              turn away if they asked for a ball
                              ignore their taunting and cussing

Then she was gone and they grew up and moved away.

IV

Spring was planting time
                  He sometimes wore her hat
                              when it drizzled
                  he would smile and remember
he watched and watered and snipped and cut and dug and turned the dirt
   moving bush to plant to plant to plant to other bush
   keeping the fertile fertile for her   he sang to the plants but really to her
   talking to her about what to put where and what needed trimming
   trusting she would answer at each and every idea
for years
Then one day a ball
   Brand new, hard wiffle, black electrical tape around it in two crosses
   No one around in the alley or yard
   They didn't live there anymore, and neither did they two doors down
      The neighborhood changed and a new family moved in
      Oh, yes, they were three boys
            and they played in the alley
            he had barely noticed   but they seemed nice and said hello
            one day he saw the oldest mowing his front lawn

but he wasn't dressed yet and couldn't stop him or say thanks or pay him, gosh he
meant to

V

It took two hands and careful steps to just walk next door and ring the bell
   while holding the covered box
When their mother answered, they hid in the kitchen, peeking
   except the oldest   sorry, sir, that's our neighbor Ma'am, we lost a ball
   in his yard   we didn't know what to do   or say
   so we did nothing   so we just played with our other ball
   we just have the two and now one
Mother said, I hope they not a bother 'cause we taught them to be neighborly

He said, please, no, they're wonderful
They're polite   and respectful   and thanks for mowing the lawn
The box is for the boys
C'mon, boys, the man says he got somethin' for you, don't be playing shy
   The oldest led them out
   The youngest opened the top and took it off
   The middle one said, "Wow!" the loudest

At the box full of 73 balls, all shapes and sizes in all conditions
   Just for them.

TEACHER

The desks were always lined up in perfect rows with the front left corner on the
edge of the corresponding correct tile
"Order to the chaos, folks."
When the board was blank, it was wiped perfectly clean
                 it was rarely blank
There never seemed to be a scrap of paper on the floor
                 the nightly janitor's dream room
But his desk was a never ending pile of papers, stacked in different ways, with
novels, textbooks, and anthologies among the papers, everywhere
"Literature was never meant to be a neat undertaking
              neither were ideas."

He was Julius Caesar, and was killed dramatically in front of the room by the
whole class
He was Huck Finn, sitting atop his empty desk, papers and books strewn on the
floor
He was Beowulf, dressed in medieval garb
He was the Stage Manager, and Our Town was in his room.
He was Atticus Finch speaking to the courtroom
"Don't memorize characters and scenes. Learn to think!"
              and I tackled racism in my heart forever.

I wrote so many words
        they were never enough
Unless it was a poetry unit, then it was too many
Every paper returned within 48 hours
"Immediacy of feedback is the only thing your work actually deserves."
He dressed average, always shirt and tie, but by rule, not to stand out
He looked average, glasses sometimes fogged by dust, shoes unshined
His handwriting was just legible enough
                to understand the explanations of why an 'A' was an aspiration
usually out of reach. ("A begins the words 'above' and 'average' but is a measure of
excellence.")

I ached for his recognition
        for his compliments
        for his attention
almost always only getting them when I needed them most ("You are a wonderful
writer when you work at it.")
        not when I went after them. ("Sometimes you bore me.")

He read our participles aloud   and dropped an eraser on the floor when they
dangled without a sentence to live in
He jogged around the room reading aloud one of my many run on sentences
He spoke in fragments for an entire class until we wrote in complete thoughts.
He played our rock music and challenged us to examine the words and decide if it
was poetry
"Poetry is image driven. Image. Image. Image."

Graduation night, caps tossed in the gymnasium in glee, hugs screams shrieks
I shook his hand
                and noticed a tear in his right eye
"You look really sad, sir."
"Sir? Am I your boss or your father?
        I work here.   I am sad
                and genuinely happy
                and overwhelmingly proud
                and edge-of-my-seat excited
                and yes, it's possible
to feel all of them in the same moment, and it's ok, too."

As my son shook hands and took his diploma from the principal
                        I wanted to tell him I get it all now

Thanks.

PART II

It is present in the midst of everyday events.

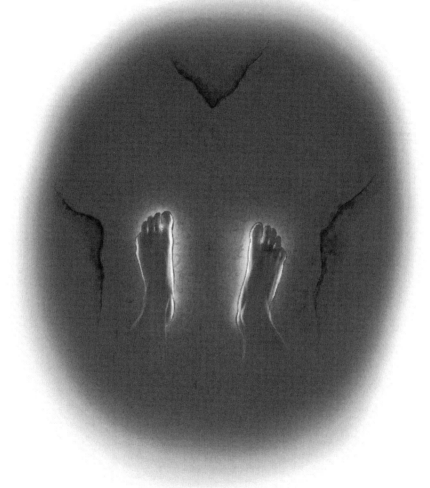

"Oldies station blasting all the way home
   Singing in the car like he hadn't in years
      Window down, blue skies, mid-70's, summer smiling

The piece of old orange construction paper, flapping in the wind
      On the passenger seat   next to him."

LOST AND FOUND

As brothers they were polar opposites
    Frank Jr. big, thick, strong, and smart like his father
    Gerald small, wiry, tough and clever
Both good athletes in different ways, in different sports
Both winners in their own ways
Both popular and outgoing, but in their own ways
    Frank Jr. by being solid and loyal and dependable and dedicated
    Gerald by being funny and crazy and kind and daring
Both off to good colleges, both predicted to return and run Dad's nurseries
    And make their own fortunes like their father did.

Frank Jr. finished in 4 years with honors with a Business degree designed to help
    Grow the family business
    Add to the family fortune
    Replace his father at the helm of the family
Gerald went a different path
    First entrepreneurship, then economics, then management
    Then 6 years and more dropped classes than finished ones
    And a particular attraction to cocaine

Family meeting, cut my ties, front me in a surfing business outside LA
    Can't miss, can't go wrong, I'll make a fortune, it'll be an investment
Dad sells part of the nursery empire to Wheeler farms to fund the dream
    No one hears a thing after six months
As if Gerald and surfing and the business and the money never existed
    No one speaks of it and slowly the elephant leaves the room
Frank Jr. manages to triple the business anyway
    As second in command, even with his aging father beginning to slip

Gerald's first rehab stint was a joke
    He bought coke from the guards
And shot up heroin for the first time on the night he signed out
    The second stint was harder
                    court forced to keep the B and E off his record
Heroin detox a pain like hell if he knew what hell was
Which he now began to think he did
Out of money led to dives and shooting houses and whoring and stealing
    To make enough for the next fix
A ticket through the doorway into hell
Rehab three no fancy frills
    The Salvation Army no lies no freedom no shit hard work
Out in a halfway house, train to nowhere, hungry, missed work to buy
    The connection lives on the block with McDonalds on the corner
Hunger.
Inside, bathroom, out and there it was
    A half eaten quarter pounder left on the table.
Grabbing it and swallowing it in two bites while barely chewing
    Sitting in the seats outside so this is finally the bottom

I'm eating someone's cheeseburger at McDonalds that they left here

I'm sick.

Frank Sr. wins man-of-the-year at the county fair for his work with the needy
    And secretly tells Frank Jr. he will be stepping down and giving him the
company at the end of the year

The walk up the long drive to the rolling million dollar driveway is long
    The truck driver dropped a ragged, unshaven Gerald there with
    "Are you sure it's here?"
He rings the bell, not feeling he has the right to just walk in
Rosa the maid answers and bursts into tears
Screaming and crying and hugs and yelling and Mom and workers and Frank Sr.
comes down and hugs his son and doesn't speak except to say sit down and eat.

The word travels through the nursery next to the house and all the workers are
eating Rosa's pancakes and eggs and bacon and sausage and...
Frank Jr. pulls his Lexus in front of the house and wonders what happened.
When he is told Frank Sr. sees him through the window shouting at the house in
rage: "How can you? Are you freakin' kidding me? How dare you?"

Sr. runs out and stops Jr. at his car
He's back   He's scum
He's your brother   He's an addict
He's here   For how long?
I love him   what about me?
I love you   it's not fair

Probably not. But it's right.

A LITTLE RAY OF SUNSHINE

Megan and Catherine were friends from the cradle
Moms at the park
                Rocking them and talking about family and future
And watching them in their inevitable first steps and falls and scraped knees and
swinging on swings and sliding down the slide and playing in the sandbox...

Megan was always so happy
It was said she could see a ray of sunshine in a thunderstorm
While Catherine was always so serious
    Even when they played with Barbies
    Catherine's Ken was always in a fight with her Barbie or some kind of turmoil
    While Megan's were always strategically placed to look as if they were living
happily ever after.

When she was seven Catherine's Mom had her take up the piano

And Mrs. Schroeder said she could play naturally and well but she was always
fighting the keys and even the simplest pieces sounded almost angry.
Megan played the clarinet, mostly so she could play something, too...
    And right away she could play big band music just by ear

Megan scored off the charts on standard tests
Catherine scored well, too, but there were always questions she erased three or
four times and probably got most of them wrong
    only because she couldn't make up her mind, and never because she didn't
know

Still they were inseparable
Where you saw one, you were sure to see the other
And Megan would be smiling and Catherine would always be in one funk or
another...
And even with all the junior high drama they rarely fought or argued
And Megan understood and just accepted that Catherine had her moods
And Catherine knew that Megan understood her
And for awhile that was enough.

Even when Megan was asked to Homecoming by a sophomore
    As a freshman
And Catherine wasn't asked
    They told each other everything
And if Catherine was jealous it never showed.

It was mid-sophomore year when the trouble happened.

Catherine wasn't herself and Megan knew she was cutting
    tried to get her to tell someone, anyone
But it was a secret and best friends don't tell.
    it was late at night and Catherine stopped texting

She usually did when Megan said nice, happy things that had compliments about
how Catherine looked, or told Catherine nice job on the Bio test, or she heard her
play in the music room and she wasn't really punching the keys any more...
But this time Megan sensed something was different and very wrong.
And she acted on a whim and climbed out her bedroom window at 2 a.m.
And sneaked down to Catherine's house and climbed up to her bedroom window
and slipped inside...

The empty bottle of pills was on the nightstand and she lay there looking peaceful
and resting, but Megan took a deep breath
and checked and noticed the bedroom door was locked and called 911

And all hell broke loose.

There was an ambulance and stomach pumping and yelling and hospitals and
therapy and medication.

One day late in junior year Megan heard someone playing beautifully in the music
room
And she knew it was Catherine
And she stepped in and they smiled shyly at each other.

Megan was the President of the class and then the Valedictorian
   Graduation day brought a monsoon with thunder and lightning and mud
But it didn't matter as Megan was called to the stage and spoke
About lifelong friendship
               And the beauty of the gift of it

During the standing ovation that followed
As the thunder rumbled and roared outside
   the rain pelted the windows of the gymnasium
Megan stood at the podium in tears, flashbulbs popping, the cheering sincere...

She stole a glance to the end of the third row of graduates to her right
Where Catherine's seat was empty
   Because she was standing and cheering and crying
     their eyes met
And they smiled a knowing smile to and at each other

Because a ray of sunshine came through the gym window
That only the two of them saw.

DISEASE

He stood outside the crowded bar and took a deep breath
   Friday, early evening, music blasting, laughter, dancing, smell of pizza
   He knew this was not an advisable step in a step by step process
      But it seemed to work for him.
Last Friday if he did this there would have been no pause, no deep breath
   He would've cashed his work check and stayed the weekend
     In the same stool   if he didn't fall onto the floor   if they let him
He was lonely last Friday
               And feeling the sick
                  and the shame
                  and the what's the use   or worse
the difference
   so he went to the 7 o'clock and poured out his soul
     and held steady when others poured theirs
     and called Gerry who told him the fight is about tonight
       when he told him he had ruined his marriage
           his kids won't talk to him
           he lost three jobs
           minimum wage makes the future bleak

But today he was cocky.
   He felt like he was on top of the world
      Boss gave him the easy pallets and an hour of overtime
         Even if was only twenty minutes
      The girl in the office flirted with him with double entendres
         He knew it meant nothing but it was good to know that part of him
            Worked was alive and someone somewhere would with him
               If he tried hard enough and wanted it bad enough
He could be back at it in no time, top of the world, women, money
   Who needed sleep the coke was a miracle that kept you going

This was the day he took the deep breath.

Walked in the bar
              Sat at a stool near the TV, Sportscenter on, no one watching
Ordered a club soda with a lime, on ice
   Strange look
      2 dollars, really?   Whatever
             Heart pounding quickly
             Cold sweat
             Hands shaking
             Sweat actually dripping from his forehead
             Sweat in the armpits, the wrists, behind the knees

"Sir? Sir?"
"Huh?"
"Sir? Are you ok?"
"Yes."
"You look sick."
"I am."

He struggles to his feet, stumbles to the door, spins and takes a last look

   Out the door into the street, breathing in the cool air
      There, there. Now it's ok. Heart slowing down.
      Never again. Never again. Never again.

Until the next time.

DRAWER

The week after the funeral
   The call came from the oldest brother
      Hey we have work to do we have to clean out all our stuff
         and divvy up theirs
I got my stuff out long ago before I got married before they moved
         No, there was a drawer
Huh?

She kept a drawer in the old dresser in the garage

Huh?

It's all your stuff, there's a college graduation program
Your name is in it it has to be yours

The same train stopped him, the same lights, the same turns, the same
Car automatically pulls into the drive, right side to leave room   for

Key, sun glare through the picture window, musty, smells like   old
Dust   floors clean   tables clean   counters clean   dust
Into the garage what dresser did he mean?   Oh that one
All these drawers are empty   oh that one

The graduation program   distinguished, high honors
Gosh that mattered so much then
A Hawaiian ash tray   brought back as a gift by Kim on her senior trip
Kim
Deserves a line of her own   oh, the trouble she caused
5 garters from 5 dances homecomings and turnabouts and proms
A rock, paper weight size, Indiana Dunes
Old Grandad Whiskey bottle, that must have been a night   or two
11 holy cards from 11 wakes
8 wedding invitations   worth keeping   the ones that cost him a tux rental
Thank you card from the Pee Wee team   thanks for coaching us
Too many pictures   of too many people   he didn't know   any more
Softball team shirts   and trophies without labels   but he won
The varsity letter that never made its way onto a jacket or sweater
4 cigarette lighters   all still worked   must have meant something
At the bottom of it all
Out of place construction paper   orange
With blue and purple and red crayon
Colors didn't mix   picture of stick figures one tall long hair
one short no hair
both smiling
"Your the best mommy in the hole wide wulrd."
And a kiss in red lips that were hardly size appropriate.

The items filled the cardboard box
He had brought along
And he duct taped it shut
And he placed it atop the trash bin on the side of the garage
Box full of other days   other times   other people
worth the drive   and the smile   though

Oldies station blasting all the way home
Singing in the car like he hadn't in years
Windows down, blue skies, mid-70's, summer smiling

the piece of old orange construction paper, flapping in the wind
on the passenger seat   next to him.

41

DRESSING AND GRAVY

PTSD.

He smiled and wished he knew what that was before 2009
                                    before 2 failed marriages
                                    before 3 trips to rehab
                                    before 7 total nights in jail

He pulled his Taurus into the community center parking lot
                                    it was nearly empty he was early
he could help prepare the meals besides serving them but he liked that the best.

Jenny liked it that he did this   she didn't mind Thanksgiving without him
Since he reconciled with Julie and Billy they didn't understand
            but were ok if he got over there on the weekend to see their kids
                    the kids loved the crazy Grampa with the beard
                    who drove a motorcycle even in the rain
                    who wore the army clothes and wore the medals
Kimmy didn't much care either way
  because she never forgave him
and he was ok with that   because he really was mean to their Mom
            and forgiveness is hard and took him a lifetime
and still the demons would pop out sometimes and he'd have to deal.

He got to work in the kitchen   mixing greens   opening yams   cutting turkey
        And what he liked most   stirring gravy   panning the dressing for the oven
He had to wear the sterile cap on his head
    but he chose to wear it over the hat   'cause the hat said Viet Nam Vet
                    and that's why he was here
for the past 5 years   on an idea from a therapist who told him about PTSD
                            made sense of the nightmares
told him why he jumped out of his chair when the phone buzzed or doorbell rang
        that forgiveness comes from inside not out
        that he was mad at the world because he was hurt by the world

You're a baby killer!
With spit, and thrown soft drinks and coffee and French fries
        As he stepped off the plane, fresh out of country   home
Again and again and again   you're a baby killer!
It would sometimes go away about two thirds of the way down a bottle of Jack
        Then it would come back louder in the morning
        And he would scream and yell and throw whatever was handy
            Sometimes the bottle   usually at someone
            or swing or kick whatever or whoever   a cop, a person yelling
or his wife.

They were shooting us from the hut, killing us from the hut, blowing us up from
the hut, my friends were dying and their legs were gone and their arms and their
faces and yes I blew up that hut and everyone in it and kept shooting at it even

42

when it was just burnt rubble and yes there were babies in it and they're dead and
I did it so yes I'm a baby killer – pass the Jack.

Then the little old lady   from the hamlet   Thanksgiving 1970
            She saw me and knew me   she was afraid   I might go off on her
Staring in a mindless haze, drunk, C-Ration turkey meat in a can
            Laughing a mindless laugh at turkey at the end of an army issue fork
She is next to him with a plate and she kneels and hands him a plate
            Noodles chopped up in vegetables and covered in a brown in a brown
In a brown   gravy of some kind.
She takes the can of turkey and pours it on the plate
      Mixes them up in the gravy and noodles and vegetables
            Her English is badly broken but still, "You eat. Turkey and gravy and
dressing. You Americans. Happy Thanksgiving."

And he loses that in a river of 40 years and Jack Daniels and lost jobs and
alcoholism and meetings and violence and tears and and and and and PTSD.

Then he finds it in a therapist's office in 2009 and cries for 4 days straight.

He stands in the line each year   hat proudly on   helping pass out Thanksgiving
dinner to homeless and poor   his station is the dressing and gravy   they like
him as they pass by   he is always smiling and he gives extra helpings.

FLAT TIRE

She knew him as well as anyone
      17 years of marriage
      6 children, a 7th lost at birth
      Oldest living through an 18 day coma after an accident
      3rd with leg braces and walking trouble and the fear of polio
      2 jobs, a house, a car, 6 Catholic school tuitions

He was big
      In every way possible
            Physically strong
            Loud
            Temper
            Rascist
      Every party, picnic, holiday celebrated
            As if it was happening for the first time

When he raised his voice the viciousness scared anyone in the area.

It was the time of white flight and neighborhood change
      Their family was leaving their block and bungalow in a few months
      Bigger house, safer schools, more places for kids to play...

The car turned onto the side street toward home
   Car packed with groceries, a task for just the two of them
      The disabled car, flat tire, black man, shaken, having trouble with the jack
      Wife and two little ones inside, in tears
Crowd of young toughs
   Across the street making trouble noise   white

She watched his face as he quickly scanned the scene
   40 years of living in these streets
She knew she saw the entire picture immediately
   As he pulled behind the flat tire against the curb.

He jumped out and quickly positioned himself
   As a threat to the young group calling racial slurs
He stared.
Silence.

She watched him walk to the flat tire
         jack up the car
         remove the flat
         put on the spare
         screw in the lugs
         unjack the car
in moments.

The car drove away in a hurry
   She watched as he stood
         and glared down the youths who glared back
            got back in and drove toward home, saying nothing.

A block from home
   At the stop sign
   As an afterthought
He looked at her and shrugged.

"They needed help."

FOG

Running on a school track late at night
         late at night on a school track running
orders the chaos
quickens the heart rate   slows the mind too busy
step   step   step   step   step
   step   step   step   step   step
around and around and around and around
   Miles.
clears the head   so the heart and soul can follow

        or maybe after the first mile
        first clears the heart and soul, then the head

From the north across the vast practice fields
   a drop in temperature
   new air on old air
   moisture in the mix
Fog.

The next lap the fog moves closer
   It lives, it breathes, it moves, it nears the track and game field
Like always in the dark, moonless night
   when no one watches   but the lonely runner step step step step

Bleacher fog track fog game field
   The fog continues to creep but moves no further
Tries, wants to, tries, wants to, tries   can't.
Game field artificial
   Temperature air moisture all present but ground fake
step step step step

Fans cheer lights on fans cheer players play fans cheer coaches coach fans cheer
   when the grass was real and there was mud and line chalk and divots
and hash mark paint
   And the fog moved in when it wanted and crept where it intended and the fans
cheered the home team and didn't create vicious chants aimed at other players
and referees and coaches and even their own team because if they let my friend or
son or brother play or called different plays or let the players play or didn't cheat
like their school always does…

step   step   step   step   step
    step   step   step   step   step

One more lap to 16 and 4 miles.

Fog invisible
       Gone but still there
             Evaporated but measurable
                    Past but present
Clear still
     but only to the lonely runner
               with a clear heart
               and soul
               and mind.

HALF FULL

2 extra hours of overtime
   This was a good weekend to get home
      Late October, spending money running out faster than last year
        So much more to do on campus as a soph   nothing is free
On the way home in a cold Chicago late October drizzle
   Her van just leaned right into his lane like that's where the road went
   She didn't brake or veer or or or at the last second he saw her texting
      He found out later it was LOL to a friend's comment   about a boy
The van hit him going 45 and his little KIA went into a spin
   Slow motion memory took over later as the spins and flips seemed out of body
      He just remembered light   flashing in different speeds and directions
      And when his head hit the driver's window
         The light changed colors   a kaleidoscope   of oranges and greens and
reds and yellows and purples and blues   and spinning
         Until the abrupt stop and pinned upside down and trying to lean
       Against the broken window pavement hung upside down
       By a seatbelt designed to save him
Blood warm in his mouth on his face in the puddle beneath him
   Trying to lean lean lean as it rushed to his head   stuck
The kaleidoscope with him he saw it and saw it and saw it as it kept changing
   So beautifully   he thought   how strange but it is
"Does it hurt?"   is that a real question? Can you really ask that?
         Oh, he just wants to know if I can feel anything.
        Yes it hurts   like I fought a battle I was never in   and lost

Then more pain and darkness until the light of a hospital morning
   Now the light is florescent blue   better get used to that   it's light, anyway
Stabbing him in the toes do you feel it do you feel it do you feel it
   How about if I stabbed you   if I only could he thought
Whispers of he's lucky to be alive   so many bones are broken and crushed
   Talk of chances of ever walking in low percentages
Weeks of lying and being turned and lying and being turned
   And visits and cards and long sad looks   of family and friends
What was and what could have been
   Coach Johnson reminding him of his speech at the awards banquet
    "I wish everyone could just plug into Joey
    A geyser of positive energy
              Too slow
              Too small
              Too weak
All world running back 4th and 1 on the goal line for championship
           Just threw his heart at him   no gain."

Rehab.   We don't know.   Your body might not let you.
   Your body doesn't remember how to do any of this   like walk.
Mom bring my empty pretzel bin the one I save quarters in
   Cash my checks in quarters and bring them in
I'm tossing one in the pretzel bin for every workout I make it through

As he fell on his face for what seemed like the thousandth time
    He thought he should've tossed a quarter in for face falls   and got up
Again.
Bending the legs hurt so much he screamed words he had only read before
    In books assigned by someone he would've never picked up without being told
The parallel bars seemed to taunt him
    He heard them laughing each time he came in the room
                        each time he fell in between
                        each time he screamed in agony

"You can leave here when you can walk out the front door."

He made up exercises he could do in his room   as he slid out of bed
    onto the floor   where they would find him asleep in the middle of the night
    over and over   back into bed   just one or two more   tomorrow
When the visits and cards stopped he just reread them   they were still company

It was a Friday night at two a.m.
    He slipped out of bed onto his feet
    He steadied himself against the bed
    He pushed off and headed into the hall
    He walked right past the nurses' station   he knew they were watching
    He turned toward the main entrance   he felt their smiles on him
    He got to the front door   he walked all the way back
                Overnight staff cheering
Parents crying little brother and sister crying doctor crying this wasn't supposed
    To happen   to be possible   to be real

You   can   go   home   today   Joey
    They packed all of his stuff up
        9 months can accumulate a lot even in a small room
    They packed up the wheelchair he was supposed to ride out in
        "do we have everything, son?"
He looked around the room   and there it was   the pretzel bin for the quarters
    In the corner behind the guest chair
                        Half full.

IT DOESN'T LOOK LIKE YOU

We would stop doing whatever it was we were doing
    And your Dad, your Mom, my Dad, my Mom, Jeannie, Chrissy et al
"Ok. Smile!"   Snap.   Another moment frozen on film   forever   or a while
We would look later, when they would ever get developed
    And laugh the little girl, teenager, young woman, new wife, Mom with kids
        laugh   almost the same silly giggle every time   and giggle
The giggle that little girls and Moms with kids do when they see a picture
    They are in.

We would say the same things every time
    You look gorgeous   I'd blush
    You look beautiful   you'd say, no I don't, it's not natural
                        it doesn't look like me
I swear I never got it because your radiant smile jumped right out of the picture
    at me   or anyone else who looked at it

It looked like you at the campfire cooking smores at Girl Scout camp
It looked like you in my backyard 4th of July swimsuit with sparklers
    With a smile full of braces you decided to be proud of and show off
It looked like you on the first day of high school, in front of my Mom's car
    on the driveway, me looking scared, you ready to attack the world
        like you did   and you let me follow
It looked like you at prom when they announced you as prom queen
    and you jumped on stage and did that crazy dance with the sash
It looked like you at college graduation when you got your diploma
    and did that little twirl dance with Dr. Clement, who smiled and danced too
        to the roar of the crowd
It looked like you at your wedding   I swear the sun shined right through the
                          ceiling almost carried you up and out
                        of the church
It looked like you holding each of your three little miracles
    60 hours of labor total   "I guess they didn't want to leave me…"
You were right.
It looked like you at the opening of the Starbucks in the strip mall by my house
    "Ladies, may we get a picture, you two look so real, so sincere?"
        Moments after you told me it was stage four
        They didn't know where it came from
        How it spread so fast
        They'll try everything   blah blah   blah blah
It looked like you in your last Christmas card
    Family around you on the sofa in the wonderfully decorated living room
        Each of you holding a reindeer a tasteful addition
        All the extra makeup lost in the scene   it still looked like you

All those wakes we went to together
    We'd pray on the kneeler
    Deciding in whispers whether the body in front of us looked anything like
        The person we knew   even if the passing was a blessing   a no was a no

48

You gave my hand its final squeeze and I stood bedside as Dave cried and buzzers buzzed and lines flattened and silence roared but you were still there I felt you

I'm kneeling and looking down at you   best friend
I feel you kneeling and looking down on me   best friend
I've felt you here in the room all day
    and all night   and it took every bit of guts I have to come up here
    but here I am   best friend
    you're on the kneeler next to me   I feel you
    you're stifling an inappropriate giggle   like you always did
    so I am, too   like I always did

It doesn't look like you.

LATIN TEST

He lifted his head above his cubicle and looked into Darrell's
    Mentor, veteran accessible made the job easier first two months smooth
      "You wanna go to Jake's Pub after work? I want to celebrate my first
account."
    "Yeah, I was just looking at it. We need to talk before you hand it in."
      "Sure. But I did everything like you told me. I checked every line."
    "Not everything. Not every line."
Huh?
    "You have zero under internal audit/price bid check."
      "That's because I didn't do any of that."
    "Sure you did."   Giggled.   "Of course you did."   "We always do."
      "But I didn't."
    "You did."
      "I'm confused."
    "You did it. Add it."
      "That is gonna cost my account $1927."
    "And that's gonna add to all of our bonuses."
Huh?
      "All of our?"
    "The bonus pool goes up when every account does. We all get more."
      "But that's, like cheating."   He knew that sounded almost adolescent
                                         Naïve
Darrell laughed
       The barrel laugh where his head tipped back
           His mouth open   showing the thousands in dental work
   "Are you kidding? They expect it. It's what makes the world go 'round."
Huh?
    "You want to get along here? You want the other reps to like you?"
      "Of course I do."
    "Then fill in the $1927. You don't, they won't. Fill it in, I'll meet you at Jake's."

Alone at a desk in a cubicle that he just began to feel was his.

49

Staring at his family picture
    His diploma Amy's smile the World series streamer, the fraternity picture

Sophomore Latin. Mr. Sweeney. Vocab test. Unit 3. 50 to Latin. 50 to English.
    Mind blank mind blank I studied mind blank I studied oh, no!
        Friend Vince sees me in trouble signal whisper signal whisper signal
            91% but a grade next to it that looks like F minus. It is F minus.
Weird looking F.
    "Um, Mr. Sweeney?"
"Yes, Joe."
    "Um, my grade, is it, um, is it right?"
"Do you think it's right, Joe?"
    "Well I have a 91. And then I have this F minus."
"Is it wrong, Joe?"
    "Well, I have this 91."
"Yes, you do. Is your grade wrong?"
    "Um, well, yes. It should be an A minus, right?"
"Should it?"   Eye contact. Eye contact. Eye contact. Mr. Sweeney was in the
                        Mr. Sweeney was in the back of his head, behind his brain.
    "Yes."   Meekly, like a puppy who peed on the carpet   and knew it
"Then let me change it. Watch me." He changed it. "There. You happy?"
    "Yes."   But no.   And a promise that no matter what he would never
                                                            do that again
and never did.

But that was school   this was business   this was how it got done
    Everyone does it this way   all the reps would like him now
        His accounts expect it   it's only technically cheating
            The bonuses will be bigger for everyone
$1927 on the line   the bonus feeder   the real world   one of the guys

His eye caught the mirror on the corner of Darrell's cubicle on the way out.

                    He froze. Eye contact.

Filling up the briefcase he kept under the small desk in the cubicle
    Being careful not to break anything
        Hoping Mo's number was still in the phone
    Her diner still hopped at all hours
        He would need a lot of shifts and rent wasn't cheap.

GRAND CANYON

"She's gone, Mike. Get down here."
   A sister's voice on the other end like the gong on a bell
      Echoing, reverberating, bouncing and rolling and signaling an end
Without a new beginning.

Asleep on a table
   Everything so suffocating white and clean and cold
      Like her forehead when I kiss it
"She's gone, Mike."
Eyes closed, stillness, chest unmoving
   Like it would move when I watched her nap so many times as a kid
      To make sure it moved to make sure it moved to make sure

Smiling bravely, strong
   Against my own advice
Speaking eloquently, clearly without tears
   Against my own advice
            That's for them, they deserve at least this
The church wouldn't be so crowded otherwise.
"She's gone, Mike."

Move on, go forward, make her proud, work to be done, love the wife, love the
kids, walk the road, fill the time
          The years do what the years do
Inexorably and inevitably   but
"She's gone, Mike."   some wounds don't heal with time.

A ride in the mountains with a beautiful view of sunshine
        A sky only this blue this close to heaven
Some holes in the road not so deep
       even navigable in the quiet beauty of western sunset
one not to be passed over   but occasionally visited with smile and awe
like the Grand Canyon   "She's gone, Mike."

TERROR ON THE BUS

He sat unassuming
   More toward the front but more like front middle
Alone, leaned on the window wall, but legs toward the aisle
   Uninviting, hoping anyone would sit anywhere
else.

The crowd from Milwaukee Avenue piled on like usual
   Half full became near full
   But still he was alone on his two seats
   Doing the Sudoku from the newspaper
   Not looking up so no one would look down
And maybe he could stay alone
                  All the way downtown.

He knew the exact moment
     the exact place
     the exact spot
it struck him, but
         like usual
he didn't know why.

Heart pounding, body moved like a jolt
Cold sweat, terror starting at the toes and sprinting up his body
       Starting at the top of his head and sprinting down his body
Meeting in the middle and sprinting right by each other
Squeezing him from top to bottom
Can't swallow, water bottle, sip, swallow, relief, more terror
Cold sweat soaking him underneath his shirt and pants.
   Feeling beads of sweat run down his belly
          and down his butt cheek
          and down the side of his neck

He wrote a fake number in the Sudoku   looked around
No one even glanced his way   as he sat in terror, glancing at his watch
40 minutes to therapy   and another story to tell.

REFLECTION

As the toothpaste swirled with the running water
   And circled and disappeared down the drain
She dared to glance in the mirror
   And like Narcissus, she liked what she saw.

So much so that she kept her eyes there
   For more than a moment   for once
And admired the smile that stared back like a stranger

Or just an old friend she hadn't seen for a very long time.

Billy was just another crush
　　She had had dozens, maybe even hundreds
But no one knew
She had never dared to tell a soul
　　She just knew she wasn't a crush　　to them
Or anyone

Then he caught her
　　Smiling at something he said about Othello
In English class
And he looked right at her
And smiled back.
She didn't know what to do
　　She didn't even have the courage to look away
So she just kept smiling
While her heart pounded so loudly she felt they could've heard it in the hallway
　　Then she finally escaped at the bell

As she looked at her cell, at the text
　　She kept her eye on the mirror
She had spent so much time
　　Doing her hair, applying her make-up, fixing her eyeliner, her eyelashes
While avoiding looking at a face that rarely smiled where she could see it...
It felt good to look at the smile and just like it.

"You have a great smile...want to hang out tomorrow? – Billy"

She looked at it and her heart raced
　　She didn't want to turn the phone off even as she went to bed
She was afraid the text would be gone when she woke up

But as she looked full face back in the mirror
　　She knew that thought didn't take away the smile
That had pushed the everyday, every moment, now impermanent frown
　　Off her face and down the drain with the toothpaste

And swore to herself
It wouldn't take another text
From any Billy
To keep the smile there while she liked what she saw.

SHE SINGS LIKE AN ANGEL

She sings like an angel

Kathy first heard that   when she was 4
   She sang along to Disney songs on a VHS tape
   at a holiday party
   and everyone froze and listened
     and Gramma said she has the gift   and it was the talk of the family
   so she sang something at the next party and the next
Mother and father brought her to the choir director, Mr. Murphy
   Before kindergarten began
    Highly irregular   we don't do this this way   there's a process she is young
Then he heard her sing   the audition wasn't an audition
She sang Ave Maria in the church   and didn't understand a single word
   but the adult choir waiting for practice   and the teen choir waiting to leave
Froze in place and listened   to this little girl
                and asked who she was
The choir director smiled   shook his head
       in wonder and disbelief
Her name is Kathy   she sings like an angel   as if it mattered to mention that
Soon there were lessons
   and multiple choirs and churches and recitals who froze in place like the rest
    mesmerized by a child and a voice and whatever song went through her
Mr. Murphy asked a couple if they'd like to hear her
   They cried and asked if she could sing at their wedding
    She sang Ave Maria and the song finished with an audible hush in the church
     Her parents picked her up   beaming   and Mr. Murphy smiled and said
       "She sings like an angel"

School and training and voice training and classes
   Auditions and recordings and musical theater and standing ovations
Funerals and weddings and Latin and English and opera and pop and liturgical
   She sang at graduation   from 8th grade   from high school   from college
Someone was always handing her a bouquet of flowers
   She would always blush   she just loved singing
      It was simple really
Her voice coach   told her   "Kathy, you are a once in a lifetime talent..."
     " I am lucky to have worked with you."
The day she sang at her own wedding   she was a bundle of nerves
   She said it was tacky, inappropriate   no one sings at her own wedding
   James got up and asked her in church in front of everyone
    There was an audible hush   she rose and cried and sang
Those that were there didn't know whether to cry or laugh or giggle or applaud
       in wonder
So they did all four   and shared a life memory they would talk about for years
Her family   her friends   her husband   all worked, had careers, did jobs
      Kathy sang
   always everywhere for anything for anyone.

Then   on an off Thursday the morning after a choir practice
            Laryngitis   she had it before   she needed to rest her voice
                  she sprayed her throat   took a week off
                  made sure to not even sing   in the shower   or the car
Something was different   the doctor wanted tests and pictures and scans
      There were polyps   more tests   and biopsies   she would live
                        But no more singing
                  if she wanted to talk   and have a "normal" life
Second opinions   sleepless nights then weeks   begging   please please please
      facing a life without singing   Mr. Murphy   teach then, Kathy, teach.

She told the pastor she would form a children's choir
      He accepted her offer and she begged, cajoled, pressured
            any and all students in the tiny Catholic elementary school to try out
She worked at it and lost herself in it and found a group that came to practice
      They sang on Sundays and their parents were proud
It was after a Mass   a man, a woman, a little Emma   "Can I help you?"
"Can I sing with your choir?"   "You're young."
"Please. I will listen. I love to sing."   "The others are older."
"We promise she will be good, Miss Kathy."   "I'll let her try."
      So Emma sang and she excelled   her voice lifted the cavernous church
It was May crowning   the Pastor wanted Kathy's choir to sing
      He asked her for Ave Maria   Father I have no one with that range or training
      Please   "I can sing that"   it was Emma
Emma sang Ave Maria at the May crowning   there was a familiar hush
      Her parents beamed   they came to get her after the service

"Why do you cry, Miss Kathy, why? You helped our daughter so much, why?"
                  "She sings like an angel."

TUMOR

He was sitting in his office daydreaming
      Feet on his desk staring out the window at the Chicago skyline
            Thinking about how good he had it   and that he loved life
The cell phone made him jump to swing his feet and answer
      "Steve. It's your sister."   "What's up, Sis? Been along time."
      "Phone works both ways."   "We gonna swordfight? What's up?"
      "It's not good, Steve."   "What's not good? You ok?"
      "Dad. It's a tumor."   Silence.   "That's too bad. What are his chances?"
      "Slim and none. They saw it way late."   "Maybe he won't suffer then."
      "That's a noble thought for you."   "Don't start."
      "You're going to need to see him."   "Is that a law or just a rule?"
      "He's at Christ. They're managing pain."   "Can they manage mine?"
      "Ahh, now that's more like you. Of course it's about you."

The room in ICU could have been in any hospital and he could've drawn it
      Red and green lights   doesn't anyone know those are Christmas colors
      Always so dark   they need their rest   why?

Beep   space   beep   he could set his watch to it   why?
Whisper always   you might wake him   why?
It's 4:00 in the afternoon   and he knows he's dying
   Nondescript cushioned chair   another one next to it   TV on no one watching
"What are you doing here?"   "I heard you were sick."
"Sick? You heard? It's cancer."   "That's what I heard."
"That's a sentence not a sickness."   "That's a happy thought."
"It's the truth."   "You could try positive."
"I'm dying. I'm positive."   "That's clever."
"You gonna run? You're good at that."   "There it is. Your go-to argument."
"Facts can't be argued."   "Reasons can, though."
"What'd the Sox do?   "I have no idea. Did they play?"
"That's right. You're too good for Chicago. And America. How did Manchester do?"
                                     "They play tomorrow."
'Where'd I get you?"   "3rd floor. Birth and infancy."

The new pain drugs   took away appetite   brought on sweat
   Steve softly dabbed his brow as he slept   unsoundly in discomfort
"Oh, you're back."   "You're still sick."
"I'm still dying."   "You're not gone yet."
"You afraid of the guilt?"   "No. I'm a good guy."
Laughter. Sarcastic laughter from the deep inside
   Coughing fit   thrashing swinging coughing spitting thrashing
"You're so good where you've been?"   "You didn't say see you soon when you
                                     tossed me out three years ago."
"It was closer to four. Christmas."   "Ho. Ho Ho."
"Four years no call?"   "Oh, you have a phone?"
"You're my son."   "You're my father."
"You never did like that, did you?"   "You never liked me."
"Yes I did. When you were asleep."
Laughter   wheezing   coughing spitting   laughter
                                     "Why call for that?"

3 am. Friday.   Most moments are short breaths and sleep.
   Steve sits alone   staring at nothing   wide awake and sound asleep
              in memories   of catch and birthdays and Halloweens
Thrashing wheezing coughing   he can't stop
   Calm down, Dad. It's ok. Calm down.   Finally   the breaths shorten   sleep
Suddenly   "You should've let me know you were ok"
   Steve was at the bed   on it   grabbing a hand
                                     "I'm sorry. I'm a stubborn prick."
Through the drug haze   and low light   and perfectly timed beeps
"Damn right you are. Best thing about you. Be good to yourself."
                                     "Dad, I'm sorry."
"Who do you think taught you how to be a stubborn prick? Let go. I am."
                                     "Not yet. Please. One more thing."
"What?"
                                     "Sox won."
A giggle, a cough. A giggle, wheezing.
                                     Flatline.

56

WE TOO WILL ROLL IN

75 degrees and sunny with a high blue sky
   Atypical for October, but a loving Spirit has a sense of humor
      And he would've liked it, because there wasn't much breeze
         His drives would stay straight and his irons true.

After 86 years he had that coming, someone said with a wry smile
   And an attitude typical for an Irish Catholic funeral.

The Church parking lot packed
   No spots open
         Cars parked in lines
            And groups
In order to exit
       The same way
          In the same direction
Every square foot covered by a car and lines don't matter
   In an order only understood by the funeral parlor employees
   With their dashboard stickers and aerial flags.

Suits and ties and dresses and awkward
   In groups like the cars
         Scattered outside the doors and lines don't matter.

The hearse and limo pull up
   Like the whistle to end recess on a crowded school parking lot
   All herd toward the doors without being told
   Mindless meaningless, passing the time chatter ceases
Shirts retucked, ties tightened, dresses smoothed.

10 grandsons place the box on the wheeled cart
   Tears and an audible gasp (or two) and all follow in silence
   With casual whispers and hey, remember her?
         Wasn't that him?
         He used to work with his son
         Wow she got older
All stop in a dutiful moment
   As the filing in continues
          Eyes down, thoughts miles away
The prayer stops them all   and, with a short sprinkle
        The procession continues
Its relentless march   to the front
Step by step   behind the rolling box
And quiet sobs   and shrieks of three babies.

It's a celebration   the leader says
He wanted to go   we can be happy
The quality was gone   it's ok not to cry
       We can be happy and sad

Readings and songs and faithful prayers
              And can we fit all the grandchildren in the service?
The Homily about a man who loved life (and life loved him back)
          The Eulogy neatly tucked in there
            Like it fit naturally
By a son with memories and laughs   and tears
              He was my hero

"It is right to give him thanks and praise"
   Sounded right   but not
   Said loudly in response anyway   a hint of a smile from the leader
   Who knows the truth about weekly attendance
And even as a guest in the parish
   Can guess the parking lot won't be so crowded
This Sunday.

The Sign of Peace a party
   A party of hugs of laughs of tears of whispers
      And sighs they know it's almost over.
"Our Lady of Knock" fills
   And haunts the room like the incense that follows
   As if sewn and sown not sung by a grandson fighting tears

That incense dancing around the box
   Before it leads everyone out
              And they pause
Dipping their fingers in the font grateful to have something to do with their hands
   They look around   we all do
We know the smell   we sing the song   we forget some words
We laugh the laugh   we cry the tears   we smooth our dress
          And know

We too will roll in.

LITTLE VICTORIES

She circled the parking lot three times
   There were ampler spots
But she wasn't thinking, and three is three.

It wasn't hard to walk in, check the office directory
Walk out, look around, walk back in, use the women's bathroom
Walk back out, get her purse from her car, and reenter

She spun the Bic pen attached to the sign-in clipboard three times
   Then signed in
Making sure all her necessary info fit on the first three lines

Her heart was pounding, she was sweating profusely
    She breathed deeply, eyes closed, and calmed herself
Concentrating on her breaths, and breathing in threes.

When the nurse put her in an observation room, she sat her on a table
    When the nurse left, she jumped off, smoothed the sheet 3 times right
And three times left, and immediately felt herself calm down.

When Dr. Hagen introduced himself and shook her hand
    She held on for exactly three shakes
All the way up, all the way down.

As he tested her blood pressure, he mentioned it was a bit high
    She swore at herself silently, using two unprintable adjectives and a noun
And told him she hadn't been in a doctor's office in 18 years.

His response surprised her: "Your therapy going well?"
"Huh? Yes, how did you ..."
"You're winning. You're here. Now forget everything else and just smile."
So she did.

PART III

It is present in our interactions with others.

"Why don't you just give up on me?"   "Why don't you?"
"I won't I can't I never will."   "Neither will I."
"They did.   When they were done screaming at me
                                    and my brothers
                                    and each other
     I was worthless and would never amount to anything."

Silence. Total. Peace. Still.   "They were wrong."

OF STARS AND MAGI

He left the office on Friday in a hurry
    Kids have to go here and there and wife only has two hands and one car
    Tomorrow is food sorting and loading and giving
Lots on the mind and the coat an afterthought and unzipped and
    A cold November wind finds the opening and almost unbuttons his shirt
    To slap him with a chill he knows so well.
It's after 6, so he looks on autopilot to the sky and finds the star
    Like always, right there in its permanence like last year on the first November
       Night he forgot to zip the coat
                    And each of the previous years, too.

Christmas music on the radio, train at the usual place, wandering
    Same November sky same November cold same November star
       But rural Indiana but thirty years before but next to Dad but on the farm
"This pile of wood will give us five more bundles, son, if we just keep chopping."
The irony of chopping wood to sell in bundles to pay a heating bill not lost on a 12-year-old boy
    Gnawing hunger from leaving the table with plate emptied but not enough on it
    Gnawing fear that there won't be any food instead of not enough
    Gnawing pain at an innocence lost when Dad's job went on vacation to India
"What're you looking at, Dad?"   "The star."
"There are lots of stars."   "That bright one, to the right, off the center."
"Why?"   "Mom spent $1 on a chance for $100 at
                    Sullivan's."
"We don't have a dollar."   "Yes we do. We have ten."
"We had eleven."   "You're too practical, son. Your Mom has
                    the faith of a child."
She put the $10 bill in the collection plate at church the next day
    An impassioned sermon about giving
       Leading to a loud argument between her and a hungry 12-year-old
         In the car after church on the way to Sullivan's Grocery
            Where of course she had won all those groceries.
"We had eaten, others hadn't" - her only argument – which made no sense
    To a serious minded boy carrying the world on his shoulders without faith.
The last ten years were living testimony
    To the promise he made that Indiana night
200 coming together to feed 1000 (once at Thanksgiving, again at Christmas)
    Loaves and fishes and tables and boxes and cans and turkeys and lines of cars
He ran it all and felt good that his money started it
    Now it had a life of its own, even the last two years a mid-20's internet
millionaire joined up and gave more than him
Not that it mattered.
He loved being on the team that brought the boxes to the cars
    He loved the brisk cold November evening
    He loved the memories of a child's heart in a mother's chest
    He loved the light of a bright star slightly off center to the right
    He loved the line of cars
And the smiling relieved faces of kids

                    too worried to be that young
                              humbling him as he placed the box in a trunk
making light of a moment too heavy for half empty stomachs so young

Marveling as the last car pulls away
    Mom and three little ones happy to be full that night and a few tomorrows
anyway
We had enough again, we always do, and always enough left over for even all of us

He stood by his car looking at the sky and the star and let the November wind
    Whip right through him and make him feel cold and alive
The young millionaire stood next to him
"What are you looking at?"   "The star."
"Which one?"   "The bright one, to the right, off center."
"I see it."   "Yeah. Me, too. I try to always see it."
"You don't remember me."   "From?"
"From the first time you did
this."   "Huh?"
"I was with my mother.
In the last car. We were crying.
My Mom said God bless you.
You said God had a hundredfold.
I told her I too would do this
one day. Here I am."   "God bless you."
"He already has
a hundredfold."
                        The young man left
                        The older man stood
                        and stared at the sky
                        and followed the star
                        as it did what stars do

in the timeless sky.

$4.71

As he turned his car out of the Chili's parking lot
    Another pair of dinners paid for
    Another "date" after texts and emails from Match.com
    Another dismal failure that he knew was a bust
        Before the waitress finished pouring the water
Texting was a lie and so was email because he could think of responses
    And be clever
        And funny
        And even sensitive
                        If he just had a few moments to think
Not when it was live.
    No time no answer no sound   but awkward silence

And the almost intelligible chatter from diners at other booths.

It was during these post date rides he allowed himself to feel sorriest
    For himself for his life for his situation
Always the friend, always easy to talk to, always the third wheel
                                    Or the fifth or the seventh
Groomsman in seven weddings, best man in two, usher in several more
(Always the groomsman never the groom?)
Now all those friends married, having kids
                Baptisms and barbecues and chatter about school and little league
And through it all the seemingly dozens of set-ups
    She'll be perfect for you
    She even likes sports
    She's the one
The two bedroom condo he bought with confidence was a joke
    Extra bedroom filled with boxes and old knick-knacks and pictures and
junk
        And he never even went in there and kept the door closed   storage

He needed gas Citgo open card in pump filling
    Might as well run in and grab some cereal   again   for breakfast
        Fast food breakfast sandwiches cost him the ten pounds he lost last
year
Looking at his Lexus through the window Raisin Bran on the counter lost in fog
"That will be $4.71."
"Huh?"   "You need to pay. It's $4.71." A giggle.
Wallet out, fumbling, looking for $5 "Something funny?""Sorry. It's just that you
                                    buy a box of

Raisin Bran

                                    every few days."
"And that's funny, um (name tag) Dorothy?"   "Well, you could get it so
much
                            Cheaper at Jewel..."
"Well, I'm not in Jewel. And you're not in Kansas!" (God, did He just say
that? Did that come out of his mouth) She giggled. Cute. About his age.
"Funny. This from a guy who buys his cereal in a gas station twice a week."
(Whoa! She noticed. He yelled at himself to for once stop thinking.)
"From the girl behind the counter at that gas station." (Wow. Good
comeback. Was this him?)
"Ouch. Ok, so I work three to elevens at a gas station. Gotta pay the rent,
you know? Not all of us drive a Lexus."
"Ouch back at you. At least you noticed." (Kaboom!)
"Touche'. I did. And you didn't."   "I do now."
"But you didn't. I was like a machine to you dispensing change." "Not anymore."
There was a pause. It was like the smoke had to clear to him.
    He didn't ever remember being in an exchange like this.
        He took a deep breath. "Now what?"
"Now what? Now you pay $4.71."   "And that's it?" Heart pounding, begging
himself to live and not think...
"That's what it cost."   "And us?"   "Us?"   "It's 10.50. You off in 10 minutes?"

"Yes."   He could swear she could see the sweat on his brow.

"Can I buy you a cup of coffee?" "Coffee at 11 o'clock? It's silly to drink it so late."
"You could order Decaf."
    Her smile melted him. If she needed anything else, he had nothing left.
"Yes, I could. And I will. I'd love a cup of Decaf. I thought you'd never ask."

When she got into the Lexus, she handed him a bag with a box of Raisin Bran inside.
    "You forgot your change, too. You gave me a 5. Here's 29 cents. Your total was
        $4.71."

FIRST DATE

Ok, this is good, I'm still dressed ok from the earlier date.
    I have never hated this waitress uniform more than right now.
She's sharp, I'll have to be on my toes, I like that.
    Was I too much of a smart ass? I'm always too much of a smart ass. Why?
"So, um, no coffee late at night for you, huh, Dorothy?"
    "Caffeine does strange things to me late at night."
"Really? Like what? Turn you into a zombie?" Crap, geek line.
    "No. Like accept dates ten minutes before I get off work." Oops. Kaboom.
"Ouch. Did you have caffeine earlier?"
    "I had a Mountain Dew at 9:30. I was getting loopy." He was smooth there.
"Well, if you don't mind me saying, I'm glad you had that Mountain Dew."
    Aww. That was sweet. Say something. Something. Anything. "Um, me, too."
"How long you been at the gas station?" Oh, God. Did you just ask that?
    "Good. Accentuate my positives. You're great."
"I just meant, you know, conversation." That's just so you, you idiot.
    "Sure. My career is a wonderful topic. I'm kidding. Where are we going?"
"I know this all night diner. Coffee is pretty good."
    "How do you know an all night diner? Does a person look for them?"
"Lot of late nights on the weekends, you know, breakfast."
    "Yeah. I did that in college too. Then adulthood happened."
"And you graduated and got a job." Did I just say that? She's gonna hit me.
    "Hahaha. That was funny. Really funny. What kind of place is this?"

Parking spot.

Oh my God my Mom's old rule – never take a girl to a place you wouldn't take me.
    "Is this place ok? It looks like a dump."
"Well, they have good coffee."
    "Then it is a dump. You didn't answer the question." Oh my God my Mom's old rule – never go into a place with a guy you wouldn't tell me you were later.
"Your charm will brighten it up; my company will make it shine." Cheese.
    "You practice that kind of line in front of a mirror?" He deserved it. Cheese.

"I didn't know what else to say. This place is a dump."

"Great. You ask me out and think of a dump."

"I asked you out and never thought you'd say yes."

"I never thought I would either."

"I'm glad you did."

"You already said that."

"It bears repeating."

"You don't get to repeat. It's not fair."

"I didn't bring my rule book."

"Why? Weren't you on a date before you came in for your Raisin Bran?"

"How did you know?"

"C'mon, no one wears that kind of cologne on a Wednesday unless it's a date."

"Do I smell?" Did I just ask her if I smelled?

"You smell fine. First date?"

"Again." That came out wrong. I'm disintegrating.

"First date again? You can't go on two with the same person."

"No, I know. Lots of first dates." Followed by silence? Lame. Damn. Speak.

"Well, you have guts. I usually say yes and back out."

"Guys ask you out in the gas station all the time?"

"In this uniform? No. Never. You're the first."

"Then what?"

"Ok, I'll admit it. Match.com. I hate it."

"Not as much as I do."

"I go back and forth with emails, then texts, but it seems so fake."

"Then I go on the dates, and it IS fake."

"Tonight not go well?" Am I being forward? Is this too much?

"It was horrible. Like the last dozen. Tonight was a disaster. Tonight is great."

"Huh? You just said it was a disaster." I'm lost. Where did he get a curve?

"Tonight I took you to this dump for coffee. Would you like to have dinner?"

"Now? It's late." No, silly, he didn't mean now.

"I meant soon, when you might have an evening free."

"I'd love to."

"You have a great smile, Dorothy. It's cuter when you blush like that."

"This is the best cup of Decaf I have ever had in a dump."

"Somehow I think you've never been in a dump like this."

"I haven't. I'm one for one." It was his turn to smile. And blush.

"Where does one get a name like Dorothy in 2014?"

"My Mom loved the Wizard of Oz. So do I. Oh, you blush cute, too."

FIRST DATE (REDUX)

As she started her 12 year old Taurus
   she smiled and waved
        and blushed in the darkness
                  where he couldn't see
        because he was sweet enough to make sure
her car started.

It was the best moment of the best minute of the best hour
                  of her day
                  of her week
                  of her month

She had noticed him other nights
           before tonight, buying Raisin Bran at 10 pm
         but tonight, she spoke to him and joked
and he spoke back.

She had always wondered why she was
   awkward   clumsy   so very alone   lonely
She felt knew believed
          she was more than plain
                 not ugly, unshapely, overweight

Why?

Dating sites the lies of lies
   Texts and emails and pictures
     If I can think of clever then   so can he   and he usually did
Chilis and Portillos and TGIFridays and On the Border
   2 people eating and the chewing being the only sound
     Why can't I ever think of what to say why can't he why is there no
connection   ever
        then tonight

This time she didn't let the blue uniform become the obstacle reason fall back
   She pushed it all aside   doubt fear self-loathing
   She said what she thought   without a worry or a rethought
   She laughed naturally   without analyzing his responses
   He asked her for coffee   she couldn't breathe
   She said yes   she couldn't breathe

He took her number
   and made another joke about her name   lame, but she liked it
Then, goodbye, a bumped hug in which their heads almost hit
   (both went to her right)   she could never have the storybook
but that was doubt   maybe this was storybook
she smiled into her condo lot

then and then and then oh my God oh my God and then   she didn't know
                          his name

Her stomach flipped   then reflipped   then nausea
     Walked in a dizzy stupor   fumbled with her keys
     Walked inside   closed the door   sank to the floor
          Cried at first a whimper   then sobs
punching the floor   wailing   why do I always do this   why do I always screw up

she almost didn't hear the phone buzz the text

"Sorry to text so late
Thanks for joining me for coffee.
Thanks for being funny.
Let's do dinner soon.
Sorry I didn't even tell you my name.
Hi, Dorothy. I'm Jim.
I'll call you tomorrow."   She sobbed again without control.
                          She shook and trembled and wailed again.
                          She punched the floor.
But this was different.
                     She was smiling.

10 WEEKS

I held your hand and you clenched it and I clenched back
                          we squeezed
your eyes blinked and did things and made action and swirled even
                          and the nurses said you knew
I was there   so were you
I knew   but there was so much space
So   much   space
just you and me and empty

I am alive and vibrant and reeducating again
     I have my job
        I have my husband
          I have my kids
             I have my house
                     You had those too…remember?

Your daughter has your eyes   I see you in there

You didn't look like you
     although the earrings were a good idea
          and any Irish ornament with a prayer works for me (and always did for you)
             and any Bears memorabilia in a casket is a good idea (I know, a cheap shot
by a Packer fan…)

67

we stood in a similar place looking in at my mother
    I cried, you held   as I said she didn't look like her
    I sobbed, you squeezed   as you said she's not in there any more she's out
           here with us
I believed you.

You swore at me in your living room when it wasn't you're living room any more
    They were evicting you no job no money no food no health but beer
        All of the order you always demanded and practiced and gave
           gone in piles of clothes and garbage and dust and dirt
                and empty beer cans
                I saw you in there
I know you were
    like you were in 4th grade when I needed a best friend and didn't have one
    like you were when my Dad yelled too much and you made sure I knew
                yours did, too
    like you were during one of the 25 break-ups with George
    like you were during sleepover adventures
                and the 42 St. Patrick's days I knew you for
    like you were for 5 graduations including one out of state
    like you were during my bachelorette party   and yours
    like you were for my wedding
                And funerals of both of my parents
           And the birth of my son
           And the birth of my daughter
           And the birth of your daughter
And all the landmarks parents use that lead through childhoods
              for all three
I don't need rehab you can't make me you always got everything
        you have the perfect life get out of mine
            you were in there
            I know

And the nurse said that something happened when I was there
          that your eyes were alive
          that somehow...you knew
And I knew   you were in there   And I know
         you are out here with me

Now.

CACTI

The 1985 spring break trip to the Grand Canyon
    They both were scared
    They both had dreams
    Graduation loomed   so did what if   it doesn't pan out
                                he isn't really this good
                                teaching isn't fulfilling
       what if all the late nights talking in the dark turn into memories
       of nothing but late nights talking in the dark
Singing Saving All My Love For You so loud the couple next door at the motel
    Pounding on the walls, pausing and yelling   never mind, keep singing
    And then joining in   what a night, what a trip, what a canyon.

The strange gift for a maid of honor
    Oh, the beautiful earrings, and the card in her calligraphy
    But the box   open carefully sand inside   two baby cacti
    "Go and teach, best friend. Change the world. I will be there. Not much care
                 Necessary."

Setting up multiple classrooms
    Times tables, cursive letters, famous Presidents, portable molecules
       Not much changes while everything changes   two husbands, a son
         Different photos and frames for the desk
         A never ending calendar, from a class
         A book of wise sayings, from a class
         A Master's Degree in Special Ed in a special frame   on the desk, not wall
And the repotted cacti   they grow (who knew?)   no work, no fuss, just there

The thrill ended long ago
    Maybe after writing the fourth curriculum
    Maybe after another IEP that was ignored again because the district
       just doesn't have the resources
    Maybe after being passed over for committee after committee
    Maybe after being forced out of the primary building for speaking up
But putting her in junior high in her 30th year was the last straw
    So this was the countdown year to retirement
    The limit was supposed to be 7 or 8   she had 13
It was a mix of BD, ESL, ADHD, and reading scores no one seemed to be able to find
or they were in a file in a box that was misplaced but no one seemed to know so
teach them make sure they learn national tests are in April
    She knew, in two days   because that's what she does
    2nd or 3rd grade reading level maybe two in 4th, a couple that couldn't read their
name on paper
All acted out, all yelled at each other at the world at the aide at her all the time

The principal would drop in
    And write up critical reviews   cannot control her class
                           has no connection with her students
                           doesn't seem to care

While the students ran around the room hooting some days
                              singing rap songs with dirty lyrics
                    slapping each other boy girl girl boy boy boy girl girl
                    running to the office if she tried to stop it
        Claiming she threatened them and screamed at them and swung at them
                    giggling and backing up each others' lies

So she taught   because that's what she did
        on and on and day after day
Sometimes they sat down   sometimes they did work   sometimes sometimes
The call came in the middle of class   the cell ring (Whitney Houston) startled her
    I'm sorry on a whim she took it   "she just turned from the sink and fell…
            She was gone before she hit the floor ohmygod what do we do…"
I'm sorry, class, I need a minute   tears   my best friend is gone I'm sorry class
                        tears   and memories flooding her desk
Oh! I'm teaching. The class.
        She felt a hand on her back
                        They all stood around her   concern in their eyes
It's ok, Mrs. D. It's gonna be ok.   It was Juan, the worst student, the worst home
You're gonna be fine, she's with God.   It was Maria, who read at 2nd grade level.
    You need to sit back down, class, thank you   We are going to pray
    Oh, gosh, you can't, it's a public school, I'll   We are going to pray
                        For you and your friend
            It's our idea and they ain't gonna do nothin'
No. Please. No.   They were on their knees.
            Your best friend is with Jesus, Mrs. D. It's ok.

She glanced at the corner of her desk   they had grown so much in 30 years
Prongs healthy, sharp, tough outer skin necessary
Standing tall, standing proud, inner nectar ripe
Just sand, some light, an occasional sprinkle

            Cacti.

ALWAYS THE GOOD GIRL

Her Godfather was a scientist
    And he always said her body had to be a dopamine production center
Because her smile was constant
    And it reached the dark recesses of any room she was in.

She kept her VHS Disney library
    In a case in the back of her closet
    With a plan to turn them into DVD's someday…
(but she had each important line memorized, so that day wasn't necessary)

Her friends called her the happy ending girl

Any book, any show, any movie – a "classic" as long as the right two end out together in the end...

Two bookcases full of Harlequin romances and their lesser known cousins on one wall

A non-Disney DVD case in the corner...all with happily ever after inside
To fill up the occasionally lonely night when her faith faltered and she needed to believe.

She got her friends to work the food pantry, PADS, the soup kitchen...
Everyone should eat and have a place to lay their heads

It was a soup kitchen night her junior year that woke her up to herself
He would've been cute...if he weren't so grungy, with the dirty jeans and sweatshirt with old paint and torn jacket and shredded White Sox cap, hanging sideways off his head...and he had energy....and warmth...and was grateful to all...and helpful to even those others he didn't know
Who were there with him.
She shyly served him
And remembered her heart racing, and sweating just a bit, and him joking with her, and her saying, "You have such positive energy...for, I mean..."
"Being one of them." He finished her thought as if he helped plan it.
She blushed then stammered but nothing came out then blushed...
"It's not always gonna be like this for me
I appreciate your time and service and the meal...but not your pity
I don't need it." with a smile that wasn't meant to bludgeon...

Eyes wide open after that night
Heart in each moment, in each gift, in each service trip
Appalachia, inner city Cleveland, an old slave house in Mississippi
Into the streets of Lincoln, and Omaha, and Dubuque

Service and awards that didn't matter to her
  And a sorority that did with friendships that fed her
  And a degree that meant something
Teaching (of course)
        So she could spread the dopamine drip that ran its natural course
through her veins.

Dates and even boyfriends (one for over a year)
But never the thunderbolt she dreamed of
        After her first (and only) opera
No Disney or story for the DVD rack.

Still the nights of popcorn and happily ever after movies alone in her apartment
  Helped get her through as did all those wonderful little students every day...
But she must have known she was lonely
  It took her weeks to put together the Match.com profile
  And more weeks to pick the right pictures
She didn't tell a soul, not even her BFF...

"Let's meet for a drink."

"Ok!"

"I might not look so good, it's after my softball game."

"That's ok...still sounds like fun..." and then butterflies she hadn't felt for years.

He's a lawyer, he's cute, he's self-confident...why me?

Why is he on Match.com?

When he got to her table he knew her right away...

"You don't remember me, do you?" he said with such confidence...

Then he turned the White Sox cap on his head ever so slightly and she blushed as if Pavlov was at the next table...

And he reached out, grabbed her hand in his and kissed it...and said

"I dreamed of tonight since I was in high school..."

And she floated into the Disney VHS playing in her head.

COUNTRY SONG

At 5:45 am the twanging of US 99 begins as the alarm on the clock radio
    On her gramma's bureau which lies within
        Her right arm's reach   from her pillow

She gently hits it off and climbs into her momma's robe and slips into the kitchen
    So as to not wake him just yet   he can use the extra 15 minutes
            His days are shorter but his work is harder
            She smiles that she knows that
    Her days are busier   her work is demanding   her work demands the patience
        Of the angel he gave her for their 5th anniversary   that sits next to
the radio
            On gramma's bureau
What he does with concrete cuts him and cakes dirt on him (which he
hoses off each night   like he was a steer) but he wouldn't come in her
back door dirty
            He never did.

Eggs in the skillet   toast in the toaster   cantaloupe sliced like the kids like
it
    Radio on the window sill playing softly
                            All that started before one song
ends
That Miranda Lambert one she sang at the CMA that he danced with her to
    In the living room after the kids went to bed   what a night that was
By 6:15 he's in the shower and the kids are rubbing their eyes and saying
can't today be Saturday
And she smiles 'cause now the day is going and the house is shakin'
                    Eggs out of the skillet and in goes the bacon
Momma taught her long ago that timing's what makes a breakfast special
And she wants to turn the George Strait song up but realizes she knows all
the words   and doesn't need George to help her with the bacon or

the song

School bus gone by 7 and an empty house and a ten minute break
Coffee and a plan and laundry and cleaning and weeding and taking care of
the dogs
She smiles when she's out there and knows that's when she remembers

It can never work   you're just outta high school   you've never known another
boy   you're not even old enough to drink   just give the baby up   he's not the
college type   you can't make ends meet   what happens
when his pick-up truck hits 200,000 miles   hauling heavy ain't a life for no one

They just had each other
                    Christmas was empty and cold
She waited tables at the diner
                    He took anything anyone would ask
Then she had the trouble and was in bed
                    And he sat in her gramma's rocker and played his 6
string
And he sang softly
                    And she sang with him
He could pick up a tune the first time he heard it on US 99
                    She never played another station again
And had two more kids
                    While his work picked up
The Millers loved him and just about gave him their place
                    When they moved to Oklahoma to retire with their
kids
And she made it a home that surprised her Daddy and made her Momma proud
                    And he worked and fixed it up and on a Friday once a month
He took her dancing up at Billy's Barn and one night he surprised her

It was an open mic and the owner Billy brought up his 6 string
    He had it hidden there the whole night
        He sang a love song he had made up long ago
            In a room where they had nothing and she carried both of them
He sang happy anniversary and family and friends all cheered
    He sang she was the one and the reason that it worked
        He sang he fell in love and he knew the moment and the time
            He sang it in a song he could in which shakin' and bacon rhyme.

ANGEL

Even now in the hell of darkness and searing pain
    The events were all jumbled and out of order
       In focus but out of order   maybe   he couldn't tell   it happened fast
    There was no slow motion in the replays in his mind   just skipping
       From moment to moment front to back end to beginning middle
Beth's house bonfire finally she liked him Joey said so Carrie told him
                                     Beth and Carrie are BFF's.
Playing it cool, laid back   but Beth's little 4th grade brother was like a fire
nut
      Throwing paper in and other stuff and garbage and told to stop ten
times
               And then ignored which was what he wanted
His name his name his name   Mikey   Mikey stop Mikey don't Mikey
please
    Then Mikey tossed the gas can in the pit on the fire   there was a
moment
    But it wasn't slow motion   but it was frozen motion   time stood on its edge

Whoosh   like a fireball but not like one because it was one and he knew
       In a second he was on fire   like he was in the pit
       But now the pit was out here   and it was on him   he was in it
Screaming (his?) screaming running screaming   OHMYGOD
    Stop drop roll stop drop roll stop drop roll   it took four or five rolls
      Before the fire went out   the last two rolls hurt like hell   he knew
that
The screaming continued   he didn't know who it was   was it him?

Someone telling him to breathe calm down breathe please calm down
breathe
    From inside the sirens   they weren't coming   they were there and
gone
He was with them   there goes my chance with Beth   he thought he
smiled
    But wasn't sure he did because he couldn't tell if he could
Breathe. Mask on   then the smell the awful smell make the smell go away
    But no one did   it wasn't until a tomorrow he knew it was him

He slept but didn't sleep or did he the throbbing never stopped nor the
searing burning pain feverish sweating but then very cold and then the scrubbing
of the burned areas and someone was screaming and it sounded
like him but he never screamed so loud for so long so he wasn't sure.

The voice was soft and high
    a cross between the fairy godmother   and Mrs. Doubtfire
he first heard her the first wrapping   and first scrubbing   and first icy
sweat
    it seemed she was there for the second and third and fourth and after
she never missed   his eyes were covered   night nor day   he just knew

that voice was there soft and gentle and sweet like her touch even
when she had to hurt him
"It's ok. You are fine. You are going to see, don't you worry. The pain will
stop, I promise. You will cool off. You will warm up. They said minimal scarring.
We just have to hope. I'm here; I won't leave. Just sip it slowly and
let it wet your whole mouth. Feel its coolness. I'm here. I have you. You're fine."

He came to know her touch
    Her smell
        Her voice
            Her silence
                Her presence

When they took the bandages off his eyes   his terror was real   what
would...
    He didn't know the guy in the mirror   he screamed and knew it was
him
She gently touched his arm as his parents wept silently
    "Time, my child. Things take time. Patience. You are beautiful. You still
are."
Wrap, scrub, shots, drugs, wrap, scrub, wipe, dab, soft soft soft touch
    Physical therapy living hell   first two steps are the biggest
        She would say each time they came to get him
Walk to your bathroom, go by yourself, walk back to your bed then you can
go
                        Home
He did that   and   slept through half a night   without waking up
screaming
    She softly applied the salve   when the itching took over when the
burning
        Was on break
                        Home
And wrapping his stuff up and in the chair being pushed out by an orderly
    Past the next room in the burn unit   curtains drawn   door slightly ajar
        Young girl crying in a hopeless wail
            Then the high voice
"No, my child. You will be fine. I'm here. I won't leave. I promise. You'll be
ok."
    As the chair rolled on, he smiled   she would be ok   and so would
he.

3:25 TO SACRAMENTO

Danny was always a dreamer
    Not to be an astronaut
            or a baseball player
            or the President
    instead to be different

75

                    pilot a one man sub
                    hike the Pacific Coast Highway
                    replace the coral reef
His Dad told him dreams are great but only dreams
     Without education   so DePaul
     His major was ecology   he wanted to know how the world really works
His roommate, Zack   and friends on the dorm floor
     Loved him   he was delightfully off the wall
                         They invited him along   college parties

Thunderbolt   right in the middle of one   she stood
                                                            smiled right through him
"Hi, I'm Danielle."   "We have the same name."
"Your name is Danielle?"   "No. Danny. But they're the same."
                    Giggle.   All night conversation
Listening and smiling   talking and dreaming
"My major is business   I want to know how the world really works"
                    Opposites attract
Driven to make a million by 30   driven to dream why moths eat clothes
     to be a CEO   to irrigate a desert
     to be on the cover of FORTUNE   to refreeze the polar ice cap

she loved Oreos and Cheezits   he loved green beans and cauliflower
she ate steak on their dates   he tried tofu and became vegan
she told him he was a cliché   he told her she was a cliché
                    when they argued

She was recruited off campus by a corporate headhunter
          He heard of an all-natural farm in California that needed a scientist
                    Graduation
Come with me to New York   Come with me to California
I'll pay for everything   We can live off the land
You can save the world from either coast
                         You can make millions on either coast
I love you more than you know   I have never loved anyone like you

She began her job on July 1   in Manhattan
She hugged him at the Amtrak Station on June 28   though
     Green duffel bag
                    Torn jeans, White Sox hat, high top, untied Converse
She cried   as he waved   from the window seat   in the car on the train
Ticket in hand
                    for the 3:25 to Sacramento
                                        as he dreamed
                                             if there might be a way
to make drinking water   from the Pacific Ocean.

DEAR GEORGE,

Dear George,
  It's already been over a month
    since you dropped by
      on your annual visit
    that reminds me
  I wish I had you over more often
to remind me to remind me

Every year you visit
    and I resolve when you leave
  things will be different
  and I'll change
    and be nicer
And more caring and unselfish and open and accepting and thoughtful and all
around loving
    It lasts a few weeks   maybe   a month at most

You're one of my heroes, George
  Why can't one of your visits stay with me through February, anyway?

I see my books in the case
  I could take Tom Sawyer out   or Huck Finn   or Scout and Boo Radley   but I
don't

I see my jeep with 170,000 miles on it and could be glad I have it   and my house
and my health
  but I'm not

I see my aging family and I could appreciate their ever-growing wisdom   and be
more patient
  and less frustrated   but I don't and I'm not

I could look at home and see Sycamore Street and Bedford Falls
        but I often see Pottersville   and feel it, too

My movie house has the option for Bells of St. Mary's but never plays it.

Maybe I could find Mr. Welch to knock some sense into me
      or Bert to search and find the real me
      or Ernie to give me a ride to what's important
      or Mary to go back and open up my library   and keep it open

Or maybe   perhaps
I could grow a green thumb   I could plant a rose bush
And tend a garden   and water it
And give it sun   and nurture it
And feed it   and name it
                  Zuzu's Rose

and clip some petals
and carry them
to remind me to remind me
what you taught me long ago

I miss you, George. Come back soon.

DREAMER

As he sat sipping coffee, looking at the yard through the window
He allowed himself a moment's reflection
And thought about days in the past
When he would never have looked at the yard or dared sip coffee.

He thought of Mr. Cash, and sophomore English, and the short story book
And the first time he met Walter Mitty
And how they discussed how sad it was
And how pathetic he was
Because he had grandiose dreams that helped him escape from the mundane
(or painful or difficult or uncomfortable)
It was the first time he ever raised his hand in that class
(and last)
Just wanting to know what's wrong with that?
He could still hear them laughing
And Mr. Cash explaining that there are healthy ways to cope
But he never explained why it was unhealthy...

So he dreamed

When mom and dad would brutally maul each other with words he never
wanted to know (let alone hear aloud)
He stood at the plate, bases loaded, two out, World Series grand slam

When his boss was screaming at him about missing deadlines and or else
He was busy running into the end zone in overtime of the Super Bowl

When the priest did his dance around his mother's casket with incense
He was hitting a three at the buzzer of the NCAA championship

When his wife told him there was never enough money over and over
He hit a putt on 18 to win the Masters and wear the green jacket

When his daughter broke her arm, and his son tore his ACL
He sat in the hospital waiting room listening to the roar cheering him on for curing
cancer

And then the other night, he was supposed to pick up his son
And walked into a surprise party

78

For him.
The cheering was real
  And loud
  And sincere
Folks from work from church from the old neighborhood old friends wife's friends
son's friends daughter's friends siblings nephews nieces cousins
  He was surrounded
He sipped the coffee again and looked at the yard
  There was nowhere to go
There was nowhere to run
  There was no escape
  There was only
Now.

FLICKER

The moment was seared with such heat into her consciousness that she
remembered it every day
        Sometimes twice
                And on a bad day, three times
And now it was more than thirty years ago.
She was eleven, eating bacon and eggs, drinking orange juice
  Mom at the stove, asking Dad if he wanted more bacon   sure
                  Toast   sure
                  Eggs   what about
you?
She smiled, turned, and fell.
Doctors said the aneurysm killed her before her body hit the floor with a
deadened
        thud.
Misty memories of a wake, and a funeral that included her shrieking in a
haze of incense   I want my Mom!
Her father and two older brothers reaching to her and beginning years of
not knowing exactly
What to say
What to do   except be and say awkward all the time.

Years and years of power studying and straight A's and AP scholar and multiple
majors and the only B the second semester of fifth grade
  The year before   when it didn't matter   and no one noticed
A Ph.D in Biochemistry
A university fellowship   then professor   then department chairperson
  Published   quoted   respected   alone.
Not unattractive, not painfully shy, not overweight, not depressed, not ever
  (even once) on a date
College roommates brothers' wives department colleagues church committees
  On a list for Christmas cards and birthday cards to be checked off
    And to be added to next year's calendar

And every day, at one moment (or another) a slow motion replay of a body
dropping falling leaving
                    thud.

Christmas mall rush and crowds and duties and nephews and nieces
    Who are growing and bigger kids mean bigger toys
        A little more bulk means bigger bags, not so heavy but
Harder to carry   just to the escalator   then to the parking lot   then home

    Duty leads to a wandering mind
                            Planning lectures beats power shopping
She never saw the child's foot as she stepped onto the down escalator
    She knew just the slide to spice up the RNA lecture on Wednesday
Trip,
        tumble,
                reaching,
                        bags,
                            tumbling,
                                swimming,
                                    kicking,
                                        tumbling
        thud.

His grip was strong, yet tender
    "Shh. It's ok. You're going to be fine. Shh. I have all your stuff back in the bags…"
Why? Huh? What happened? I need to go. Oh my God! The pain!
    "Shh. We have called an ambulance. There's an issue with your right leg…"
Who is this? What's going on? Ambulance! What?
    "Shh. It's ok. You took quite a fall. You were out for a minute or so…"
Why the shh?   Then it occurred to her   she was not asking the questions
                                she was thinking
instead she was shrieking and screaming and crying loudly
    like an eleven-year-old.

She awoke in a room in a hospital.
    "Hi. Your Dad and brother are on their way. I just stopped to check on you."
It was him from earlier.
    "Um, well, I, well, thanks for all your help. Sorry to have been trouble…"
He was smiling.
    "Ma'am, you had a terrible fall. It's no big deal, and no trouble."
She knew he must want something…
    "I had my purse…"   "It's right on your table there."
    "I can give you some money."   "Money? Is that why…"
    "How much could I offer you?"   "I don't need money. It's not why I
                                helped you. You fell. You were hurt. It's
                                what people do. Now get back on
                                your feet soon. You
                                would've done the same for someone."

            "Maybe.   Now I will."

ODDBODY

It wasn't like she was terribly overweight
   She wasn't   and she knew she wasn't   and she knew that wasn't it
She started to notice it toward the end of 5th grade
    Well, it was noticed for her
      And once it got noticed, it was noticed all the time

Donald was the worst
   "I couldn't make you out of Play-do"
   "You should try your pants on your arms, and your shirt on your legs"
   "You're a lump then a hump, then a hump then a lump. A humpalump."
Multiple laughs every time   the humpalump stuck
            The gym teacher, Mr. Joseph even smiled at it one
day

Seventh grade   she stared in the mirror   before school the first day
        She was older   but he was still right
"Humpalump's back. Nothing ever changes."   His friends laughed
        Her friends, few as they were   watched in horror   and
terror
That they would be next
The groups began to form   she would never be cool
               she was ok with that
               she was happy she had someone to sit with
               and talk about the bachelorette with at recess
Mrs. O'Reilly liked her
   She always did her work   and did it well   and paid attention
   And raised her hand   and stayed positive   and giggled at her jokes
Even when they weren't very funny   to make her feel good
Mrs. O'Reilly knew it.

It was a Tuesday   a heavy Math day   new concepts being reviewed
   Some struggled   some hadn't tried   Mrs. O'Reilly nailed Donald
No recess   math work until you get it done   snickering   she saw him
blush
Excuse to friends   English to read   she stayed in
   Donald at his desk, sweating, troubled, confused
      "You're trying to do it all at once"   "What do you mean?"
      "You have to do the steps"   "I can't"
      "Sure you can. Just try"   "Um. Can you teach me?"
      "Sure."   "Uh...thanks."
Teaching practice thinking practice thinking teaching practice learning
review

"You did well, Donald   you can go out tomorrow"
        "Thanks, Mrs. O'Reilly!"

After the final bell of the day   Mrs. O'Reilly asked her to stay
I'm sorry, but I have to go   it will just be a minute, I just want you to

81

know
You are more than delightful   but perceptive and insightful
Helping one who hurts you is very disarming.

Walking home alone
    Book back full   slung awkwardly over her shoulders
Wondering   what Mrs. O'Reilly meant and her fuss was about
    All of those words   all of those adjectives   all of those smiles of pride
Were puzzling   confusing   hard to comprehend

She tried to interrupt and just say
        Donald needed help in Math   I knew how to do it
So I helped him.

GHOSTS

They're real. I know it. I can hear them.

School's out.
    Last day.
    Announcement, bell, whoosh!
Like a vacuum
    The air, like the students, sucked out, too.

Lockers empty, left open to be cleaned
    Garbage cans overflowing
Papers and spirals and poster board and even the odd glove and hat
    And a beaten up copy of Fahrenheit 451
And sunglasses and an old lunch and a P.E. shirt
    And team logos and motivational statements scraped and torn from the front
and inside doors of lockers

Floor full of oddities
    Index cards with scientific terms on one side
        Definitions on the other
Looking like a DNA molecule strewn across the hall
    A bookstore full of pens and pencils
    And erasers and school calendar books
And a whole dry erase board from the inside of a locker with
    EXAMS! In Sharpee across it

Strategically placed garbage cans
    Full beyond capacity
    From the assault
    That will lead to tonight's incinerator delight

Lights are on
    Sunlight through domes in the ceiling

And the door windows of each classroom
    Middle of the day, another bell
And yet silence this time
But concentration and careful listening
"Did you even finish that Algebra quiz? Impossible."
"Jamie's pissed at me. I forgot to pick her up."
"Coach said get there early if you can for extra drill work."
"There is no way my Mom will let me go."
"I got the car for Friday. We are in!"
"I knew every question on that Chem quiz. I killed it!"
"She wouldn't even look at me in the cafeteria at lunch. It's like I don't exist."

Days and months and years of hallway talk
    And bodies passing and pushing and hurrying and talking and living.

I close my eyes and hear them. They're there. They're real. I believe.

ORBITAL PATH

I can stand in the exact spot by the pond at the park near the dead oak
                    Where you showed me the north star and how to
find it
for the first time
you told me when I looked at it you might be
                    it's a big world, but a small one because we'd be as
one
looking.

I still go to the park and walk at night.
                    Especially on the cloudless nights when the moon is bright
Warm or cold, wind or calm
                    And go to that spot, and find the north star

I go to B-Dubs and order hot wings
        Two dozen, I can still do them all with the hottest sauce
        That was a great bet the first time
                Winning was never so sweet
                Collecting was delicious

I've been to 11 movies
        Most were dogs, most of them are
        But you would like Pi
                    and Mud
                        but you would've complained for dragging you to Django
Silver Linings Playbook was as crazy as we were.

I tape both NCIS's and CSI and Rules of Engagement and Mike and Molly

And Criminal Minds, too
                    But I'll never watch it Because you're not there to
be
                    scared by it, and want to stay and cuddle and not
let go of me.

My friends got me to break down and put a profile on Match.Com
    Melissa picked out the pictures
    Johnny wrote clever quips about interests and places and jobs and hopes
I got a bunch of emails
I answered a few
I've been invited for three drinks
And a barbecue
And a Cubs game
And a movie
Drew says I'm a hit; I'm on fire

Yet

Friday night I ate a frozen pizza
                    Drank three beers
Drove to the park, alone, looking at my GPS
Wondering if they have such a thing for your phone
And walked over to the dead old oak
                    Looked up at the north star
Wondering

If you were looking, too.

ROUND UP

Cindy always loved ribbon
    Especially yellow
and she tried to suppress her love of maudlin songs and movies
    but secretly the tissue was always available
    in every pocket, up a sleeve at the wrist
    In case she'd hear a country song where it didn't work out
or did.

When she left for college
    The hardest night was the last
And the goodbye to Jeff
    who was going the community college route
    who had lobbied for months that 3 years could last into many more
She cut all ties, said good-bye, this was over, they cried, they remembered, they
hugged, they stared at each other, there was silence, they cried...
She got out of his car
    handed him a cowboy statue (he loved John Wayne)

wrapped in yellow ribbon, tied neatly in a bow.

College and Masters and internships and awards and scholarships abroad
    Time, like mountain rains
    Eroded the old, the young, the structures in place
    Streams changed direction, trees fell, plants grew, plants left
Same mountain.

The job was in her hometown
    A triumphant return of sorts
    But she had only been back briefly
        To visit parents and a rare holiday
She felt she was starting over in a new town

She got out of the rental car in her parents' driveway
    Thought she'd get the bags later
        she'd go up and take a nap
        she's get the hellos and what are the plans out of the way.
On the porch by the door a small box caught her eye
    rather, the yellow ribbon tied in a neat bow around it did
It was a box of Puffs
with the word, "DINNER?" in marker on it
next to the drawing of a man on a horse
    in a cowboy hat.

SALUTE

It bothered him when she dilly-dallied and took her time
    He loved so many things about her, but that got him every time.
40 years of marriage, he never mentioned it anymore, but he really wanted
a seat in the crowded bus station
    'cause the train would probably be late and he didn't want to stand

Standing for long periods and cold, damp weather
    That's when he could still feel the lower right leg
As a reminder that he once was elsewhere
    Far, far away, in a God-forsaken rice paddy where a grenade exploded nearby.
Never thought of the place or the day, just sometimes the pain.
Because it hurt.

They found a seat and he got lost in the sports section of the Tribune.

He didn't surface until he heard the train whistle
    And, almost as an afterthought, looked at the bench across from him.
Soldier, full fatigues, large duffle bag, staring straight ahead as if they
weren't there...
Training.

As they stood he noticed the soldier wasn't
     Must be waiting for another train
     He saw the combat medal on the collar
And for the first time recognized the soldier was African-American.

Wife grabbing hand and pulling him along, hurriedly

"Thanks."

Soldier looked uncomfortably at him, focused
     Shuffled, looked down, looked up, mumbled incoherently
Nodded.

Wife, firm grip in his hand, walking through the doorway onto the platform
     He let go
     Stepped back in
And, as an afterthought
     Stood at attention
     Saluted
Eyes straight ahead, back straight, muscles flexed, face tense...

The soldier stood
     And responded with a salute of his own
Eyes straight ahead, back straight, muscles flexed, face tense...

Tears in both sets of eyes.

SESSIONS

As he sat in his KIA RIO
     windows up, air on
                         in the parking lot outside the internist's office

the feeling enveloped him like a blanket
     and blanketed him like an envelope
          complete and covered and sealed

He needed the blood work
He made the appointment
He talked to the nurse who called to confirm
                              He wouldn't be going in.

"It's an emotional paralysis."
     He heard on the blue sofa in his therapist's office
"But where does it come from?"
     As he looked at the clock and the paintings and played with the magnets
                         to avoid eye contact
"Anxiety."

86

"But why? I need the blood work. I need the doctor."
"Perhaps you feel you don't deserve it."
Clock ticks louder   or the same   he just hears it louder
Train outside shakes the windows
   It's hot, so hot he sweats, why isn't the air turned up
                  Why isn't this bottle of water cold
An hour is long so long it drags and never seems to end so long who thought
        of an hour?
"Why don't you deserve blood work?"

Shortness of breath, heart pounding, agitation
  "I deserve the blood work! You know that!"
Boiling point, explosion, spilling over, eight words flying into all corners
"Of course I know that. But you don't."
                       Gently, softly, quietly.

Tears. Always the tears. A different explosion
                the same explosion
sobbing   uncontrollable
words   indecipherable
calming   still words   clearer   "I can't I can't I can't I can't I can't!"

"Perhaps that's why you can't."

They're words   you're saying them
Just words   you believe them
I'm helpless   then you are
I'm useless   then you are

Phone buzzing on the table   he jumped in his seat
                in surrender

Ten minutes of tears   and silence
  And warm water and clock ticking and sweat
    uneven breathing and heart pounding

"Why don't you just give up on me?"   "Why don't you?"
"I won't I can't I never will."   "Neither will I."
"They did.   When they were done screaming at me
                and my brothers
                and each other
    I was worthless and would never amount to anything."

Silence. Total. Peace. Still.   "They were wrong."

KIA RIO, air on high, windows down, parking lot
  heart pounding, fear, cold sweat, short breath
door open   steps   dizzy   doorway   deep breath
"I need this."
       In.

SHELLS

The day before Momma died
    as the cancer ate her gray
        and her bones seemed to be outside of her skin
She bolted upright and grabbed the 8 year-old Johnny's arm
    alone in the hospital room   eyes staring at him from deep inside her head
        from the bottom of her sunken soul
you need to take care of Billy
    he's special   you know him
    he's different   he trusts you
your daddy doesn't understand   I'm scared for Billy
I'm scared for me, Momma   you'll be fine, son, you was born old

Billy never talked   sometimes he grunted
He watched and stared   he stopped all noises after Momma died
    He carried the marbles she gave him in his pocket
        loved to roll them and click them
        and walk with them in his pocket   click click
                        click click
always the clicking   especially when nervous   click click

Daddy just drank more and more   made a deal with the Murphys
    old screw jars filled with homemade whiskey
        for rabbits and squirrels
Johnny learned to cook and sew and skin and scrub and fish the creek
    He and Billy saw rabbit and squirrel less and less
    Daddy drank from screw jars more and more
He was mean when he got drunk   he got drunk when he felt mean
    screaming and tossing plates   back hand slapping Johnny
                across the room
    screaming and kicking Johnny
        keep the Idiot away from me
          Johnny lie on the floor in pain   knowing Billy was hiding
wide eyed in a corner, under the bed, in a closet, behind the couch
    click click   click click   click click   click click
he'd find him wide-eyed huddled   after he cleaned up
Preacher Summers noticed bruises   confronted Daddy
    I didn't teach the boy to be clumsy got that from his Momma's side
             and beat him later for talking to the Preacher.
Johnny you can get out of there   Momma told me to take care of Billy
You're 11, he's not your responsibility   I'm his brother I'm all he's got
He won't hurt him he never does   he's got me to hit
He knows he's special   he calls him the Idiot
My place is near the creek you fish by the woods your Daddy hunts
    He said that in the chapel at the lectern after services
        In front of the choir seats that sat empty   voice echoing like a hymn

Drunk back from hunting   skin these squirrels
I'm cooking fish for dinner   skin the squirrels

The fish will burn   the butt of the shotgun at the base of
his neck
        Get up off the floor   skin the squirrels   get the Idiot to cook the
fish
You need to stop hitting me   what did you say?
                broken whiskey screw jar, right hand
Stop. Hitting. Me.   You gonna cut me?
              Click click   click click   from the corner by the end
table
You're hurting me.   (Shotgun up. Pointing.) See this?
You'll rot in prison.   They'll never find you.
                                     No one knows that creek like I do.
They have dogs.   Your scent will end at the water.
                                     You and the Idiot will be gone.
                Click click   click click

After Daddy passed out the next night after dinner
    Johnny sneaked around the house
        Finding all the screw jars
        Pouring out the whiskey
        Filling the sink with moonshine
As he finished a loud boom, something fell, the end table
    Next to the couch Daddy slept on   someone tipped it over
    Daddy jumped up   click click   click click
Goddamit! You stupid sonofabitch!   the corner didn't hide him
Where's my whiskey   I poured it out
What? Ok, fine   he grabbed the shotgun and pointed it at Billy
          Click click   click click
Johnny stepped in front of Billy
    You think you're gonna save the Idiot   Ok. You first.
He cocked the shotgun and pulled the trigger   nothing
                Misfire.
Johnny grabbed Billy's hand
    Run Billy run   out the front door
    Don't look back   Daddy fell over the couch
    Faster Billy, to the woods   You think you can hide in there?
At the creek in moments
    We have to get across   Johnny couldn't get Billy to hurry
          Click click   click click
    He'll hear us, please Billy
          Click click   click click
Billy just stared at Johnny   and they were across the creek
Knocking on Summers door
    Hello, come in, I'll call the police
    You can stay here for now   you did the right thing
Johnny shook and cried and said the shotgun misfired
    Shook and shook and cried   I was watching myself die
Click click   click click   Billy stared at Johnny
Looked up at Preacher Summers   back to Johnny

Took his hand from his pocket for the first time
and placed a handful of shotgun shells on the table
and nodded his head up and down
in Johnny's direction.

THE AGREEMENT

Getting you back on those L tracks
At that specific stop
At that time
Took precise planning
And a lot of help from a lot of people
And a whole lot of ignoring the "why don't you just"" question
That literally everyone seemed to ask

It was really cold that night
Wow cold, below zero cold, bone-chilling, dangerous wind chill cold
And you're out in just a coat and scarf?
Human hair does not a hat make (someone must have said that)
You were shivering, my hat was warm, my hot chocolate was hot...
And, well, chivalry is not dead
It took you less than half a second to take the one and sip the
other
Then you talked and talked and talked as if you had to make payment
I listened and listened and listened to accept it
(all the while praying the train derailed near the Loop)
I was numb maybe even delirious because you couldn't be talking to me
My hat looked cute on your head and over your left eye
But, I admit I didn't expect you to guzzle the hot chocolate

You haven't stopped talking for two and a half years
You'd still look great in that hat but you haven't worn it since
You're a hot chocolate addict (who drinks it in June?)
And I find myself looking around   still   wondering
Is she really talking to me?

The co-conspirator list to get you to this spot is endless: both sets of
parents, your boss, my boss, your sisters, my brother, your niece, my
landlord, a host of our friends (most of them waiting at Jake's Tap for the
outcome)

You're there and you don't see me   you're so beautiful when you don't
know
I'm in front of you in the rush hour crowd, a nervous wreck
I'm on my knee, I have it rehearsed and push myself to look up and speak
I can only see into your right eye
Which is gushing tears
I can barely speak

But you somehow hear, and somehow know
I can only wonder
Where have you been hiding my hat all this time

As you say yes to forever.

THE KICK

She sat in the bare office
Two chairs, a couch, a table
And felt cold, and wondered if that was her, or the temperature
Or if all nightmares like this were scripted
And if clean and antiseptic, and the promise of germ free meant warm just wasn't possible.

She remembered how much fun the party was
At the beginning
Even in the middle
Before the last shot of schnapps took effect and she became a predictable statistic
She had dreamt so long of getting with Joey
All that energy
All that magnetic charm
All that perfect smile and wondrous, athletic body
That made him the star of every team he was ever on
And her dream that bordered on obsession.

It wasn't supposed to be like this (or that, either)
She was sketchy on the details but remembered she liked
The flirting the kissing the promises the attention
But his hands were everywhere and she couldn't keep track.
He was on her and she could smell him and she felt oddly nauseous
And she remembered clearly it hurt.
But she didn't say no.

She dressed extra special that Monday
Ellie said she never looked better
she walked by him after first period where she knew he'd be
he walked by, too, like there was no one there.
No nod, no hello, no hey I recognize you from the sex the other night
It felt like someone had kicked her in the stomach.
She felt dizzy, had to get into the stall of the bathroom
Crying so hard she missed history
Then the whispers
The pointing
The outright laughing
The headshakes and the sighing
She learned how to walk from class to class invisible
As if there was a bubble around her made of fog.

Her friends said all the right things
   He's a pig
   Typical guy
   Those type of guys only want one thing
Well he got it.

She knew pretty quickly something was different
   She didn't feel the same
   She was tired, she was emotional, she was sick.
In near terror she bought the tests and took them all
   But already knew
Then froze in disbelief for a few weeks
   Dreaming every night that it would all go away
Nightmares almost always do.

The question on the form was almost funny:
   Are you sure you want to terminate the pregnancy?
As if there wasn't already a word for this, a word she knew would haunt her
   And bring back a night she lay under a guy she ached for for 5 years.

She felt like vomiting
   And would have if the damn room wasn't so...clean.

A kick.

Could that happen this early was that real am I here oh my God it's part of me
She stood quietly
   Put the clipboard back on the shelf and the pen on top of it
   Heard questions being asked her as she walked to the door
   Opened it, didn't answer
And stepped into the night
   Didn't think about Joey, or her friends, or her parents
               Or her teachers or school or what would everyone say
   Promising herself that whatever came next
They would do together.

TWO MINUS ONE...

You said it would never work
   We were too different
   Our interests were totally opposite
   You could never really like baseball and football was barbaric
   And I'd probably sleep through the opera (and I did, more than once)

You were drinking Zinfandel
I had a Miller Lite
You said you had never seen a human being eat so much meat in one sitting

And yet you marveled that I was able to finish your fettucini, too.

You said our friends would always clash
    And never understand each other
    And put each other down
    And at parties yours would be in one room
            And mine would be in the other (close to the keg)
    And yet Beth calls when you're busy and we talk and talk and talk and
Kara, too.
    And you always manage to rib Tom the right way, and he and Rich get
you back and you laugh and it's real because I know your fake laugh like I know
your fake cry...

You said I would make money an issue
    That you didn't mind making that much more than me
    But I would soon become the caveman all men are and feel
emasculated
    And I would never appreciate the differences between nice things and really
nice things
Which was really what the caveman thing was all about, wasn't it?

You said I'd never fit into the world I'd have to fit into...
If you had a man
And had to bring one where you had to go
And my tie would always feel tighter as the nights wore on
And who would I talk to
And you would always be looking over your shoulder to make sure I was
ok...
Then I brushed my hand across your thigh when you got up to take that
call...
    And you blushed
    And you knew
    And you knew that I knew
    And we both smiled and woke up the next morning
Together.

And now we sit nine years later on a stranger's couch
    Pretending we each believe he can fix this
    Pretending we've known him all our lives
    Pretending we're all in, whatever it takes

Even though I always got along with your friends
            Your bosses love having me around
            I have three dozen more ties than I ever had, and I like them
And you still get nervous pulling into the driveways of my friends
        Or get creative with excuses not to go
        Or get hyper-sensitive about what she said or she said or she said
And they all still love you.

93

And this stranger who is valiantly trying to salvage us
                              save me
                              find you
picks tonight to: "Let's do this exercise, each of you says 'How can I...' and finishes
the sentence...
And you jump right in and say, "How can I be with a man who sleeps
through the opera?"
And you still think there are nine guys on the field in an NFL game, and you think
outs are runs, and runs are points...

And the stranger says right into my eyes, "what are you thinking right
now?"
"I want to be married to her forever, every day, the rest of my life..."
 And you reach your hand across the couch and grab mine, backwards like
you do, and smile shyly and start to cry...and say..."Me, too."

YOU'RE UGLY

I

When he heard them say it, it was at the end of a group rant
    Up against Celia's locker
He knew it was her group from Bio, because he knew their project was the best
    And they all got B's and C's because she must've nailed them in the evaluations

He saw her squirm and try and turn away
    But everywhere she turned there was one of them there
    Viciously sniping like hyenas cleaning up carcass
As it breathed its Serengeti last.

He could only listen
And pretend not to watch
But watched in fascination and fear
And pretend to continue to look for a book in his locker that wasn't there
Because that's what he did
    And he was glad they weren't on him
    For whatever reason he might be visible that day.

He was overwhelmed
Sick deep inside for her and helpless
what could he do they would just turn and devour him, too
    she was smarter than all of them put together
She wasn't ugly, either
They were so wrong he felt so guilty it was so unfair he was so frozen
    Just turning over the same notebook as they tore into her
Wishing it all would end
    Like they said it would when junior high started, and ended
                    And high school started, and now was nearly halfway through

94

But it didn't end
Carnivores need to eat and survival was accomplished by the fittest
(and the most popular, not the nerds and geeks and the friendless...
Like Celia, and well, him)

II

He remembered in 7th grade he found a pencil in the hall and Celia said
    Hey, that's mine.
In 8th grade she picked a dime up in the cafeteria and gave it to him
    You dropped this in line when you got your change
In art class last year she drew a house on his landscape for him
    That's ok, they're hard unless you know how to do it.

Finally he left the building and sat alone on the bus in the front like
everyday
and told his folks school was fine
and ate nothing really slowly
and did his chores and his homework
she would be thinking the dark thoughts tonight
    he had noticed she was wearing more bracelets on both wrists
    he knew she was cutting again...so he
formulated a plan.

III

He got up early and left early and told his Mom he had a meeting
    (Which made him smile because he was a sophomore in high school and
he had never had a meeting)
He sneaked down the alley on the block behind his, it was still dark
He took the scissors out of his backpack after he crawled on his belly into
the middle of Mrs. Hobbs' yard
It was there she grew the award winning, 100%, totally natural spring tulips
  He carefully cut three off like a surgeon
  And crawled out
  And looked back and you really couldn't tell any were missing.
  He carefully wrapped them in tissue and headed to school

He scanned the empty hallway while tearing the piece of duct tape from
the roll at the bottom of his locker (from a history project last October)
He dragged the backpack up to her locker
Looked both ways
Ripped the tulips out of the backpack in one motion
Taped them to her locker in another
And was gone, into the bathroom at the end of the hall, out of breath

He knelt by his locker, looking for a book that wasn't there
    The hallway was void of vultures and hyenas
    Just the usual morning rush before first period

Celia just stood
    Transfixed
    In front of her locker
    Staring
Then daring
    To look around, and then look around again.

She was as faceless as she ever was in that hallway
    But on this morning
    She dared a precious smile.

THE BOOK

When Kinah turned 12
    Housyar began to allow girls to come to school in Abshar
        A decision first met with silence
            Then indifference   then girls at school
Including Kinah, who would have been first if her father was not so afraid
    Of repercussions of Taliban reprisals of strict Koran translation of life
        In a village in northwestern Afghanistan   he had seen so much
                                        Already
She was near the front of the line anyway   like always
She was so bright   so skilled   so aware   so full of a sense of what's right
She could sew faster than anyone who anyone could remember
    She was a better hunter, shooter, trapper   than any boy
    She could skin, cook, sew   better than even the women
Soon she read better than them all   even the men   except Housyar
                        but he was the teacher

One day he kept her after
    Kinah, you read with such passion   I love reading
        you attack like a hungry animal   there's so much to know
        you ask hard questions   there's so much that's wrong
        you make bold statements   boys should cover their heads
Kinah you fly like a bird you are free you need to be careful   always
careful
    Here is a book   what is it?
    It is a collection   of what? It's in English
    It's poetry   in English   why me for this book?
    It's the Poems of Emily Dickinson   is she good?
    She is like you   a bird   free?
    No one ever knew she wrote   ever?
    They found her poems after she died   why?
    What's the difference   no one ever needs to know what's inside you
                You own you   your soul is your soul
                You can learn to fly inside   like she did
Kinah learned to read English   devour it really   so she could read
                Her book

96

While she tended the sheep on the hillside outside of town
While she shopped at the market, remembering to keep her burka tight
Around her eyes   and keep her head down   avoiding eye contact
"No reason to invite trouble, child"   Housyar would say
"It will find you without help"   he would repeat without a smile
Slowly she learned to read her book   and she felt she almost floated

Then the Taliban trucks came into town   unannounced
          Kicked open the doors of the school   dragged Housyar to the
square
          Rounded up the girls in the school   whose parents screamed
          Stood the girls in front   put Housyar on the bed of
a truck
          Shouted accusations and sentences   pointed a rifle in his earhole
He looked toward the girls   but not at them   smiling a defiant smile
               Yelled, "Emily Dickinson!" as loud as he could
               As the rifle fired and his head exploded
Kinah was thrown in the back of a truck
   And beaten and gang raped the first night
   And beaten and gang raped again and again
Each time they demanded she redress   burka last after
undergarments
Each time they would turn away as she disrobed
   As if there was respect   as if she were a person   as if she were like
them
Each time she took her underwear and held it tight in her hand
   On the side of the mat on the floor
      She could sew fast   and she had   into the crotch   of that
underwear
The Poems of Emily Dickinson
   They can have my body   they can rape me over and over   they can
damn me
But they cannot have my book
                         It is mine.

An Interview with the Author

Q: How long have you been writing, and have you always written poetry?

I have been writing my whole life, poetry included. I hesitate calling much of what I wrote early "anything" except practice writing. Or practice poetry.

Q: Some of your poems are so clearly written from the perspective of others. How was it getting into the minds of others, especially those experiencing difficulties, even traumatic experiences?

I have been a high school Campus Minister for 33 years, and an LCPC for 15 with a private practice in family counseling. I have heard my share of horror stories, stories filled with uncommon trauma, pain, and loss. I could only be an effective helper if I could "walk the walk" with those who were struggling.

Q: As it relates to the above question, what challenges did you face using multiple speakers (ie: young children, women, war veterans, to name a few), sometimes in the same poem? How did you work through those challenges?

At its core, a story is a story. We are people of stories – we are stories of people. No matter what the point of view – these are the stories of people. In their stories, many people talk.

Q: What inspired this collection? Where do you find your motivation to write?

This particular collection is my response of respect to those I have seen go through challenge and hardship, and those just living everyday life – who manage to do that with dignity and grace.

Q: With so much diversity in your collection, what about it is universal?

There are universal truths in every human story.

Q: Your poems tell such vivid stories, and your form (ie: line breaks, spacing, lack of punctuation, etc.) is so unique. How did you develop your voice and narrative style?

I developed what you see as style through years of practice. Of course being an English major in college exposed me to many different styles, as did teaching English. I have searched for a voice for so long – I believe I have finally landed on a voice that speaks what I would like it to speak.

Q: Why did you choose to divide the poems into three separate categories: individual people, everyday events, and human interactions?

I suppose all categories are arbitrary at their core. Some of these pieces fit into multiple places. But some tell a story by describing the images of a single person's life, while others focus on a single moment, and therefore tell a person's story. And, there are those that tell a person story by watching her interact with her world.

Q: You titled the book *The Light Within*, which has obvious spiritual connotations, yet many of your poems convey such dark, sometimes even disturbing, themes. How do you explain this juxtaposition?

As I spoke of above, many face horrible moments and life circumstances in an instant, or throughout life. I have been a witness to so much courage at a basic human scale that I believe we are all blessed with this saving fire/light that lives within us. When we need to, we can notice it and let it help guide us to that aforementioned grace and dignity.

Q: What do you feel is the biggest contribution your poems offer your readers?

Everyone likes a good story. If the story is told in a perhaps uncommon style, that experience can be both challenging and rewarding. I think this collection provides such an opportunity.

Q: What did you personally take away from this project?

I have always wanted to do this. I suppose this is a bucket-list moment. I love these poems, individually and as a group. I seriously carried them inside of me and worked on how to best put them on paper. So, I take away a sense of accomplishment, first and foremost.

Q: What can your readers expect next from you? Are you currently working on anything new?

Another collection is next. Some will be more personal; some will be darker (not all stories have happy endings.) But I want to do this again.

Made in the USA
San Bernardino, CA
13 December 2015